HAZARD

MATT AND TOM OLDFIELD

ULTIMATE
FOOTBALL HEROES

HAZARD

FROM THE PLAYGROUND
TO THE PITCH

DINO

First published by Dino Books in 2017,
an imprint of Bonnier Books UK,
The Plaza,
535 Kings Road,
London SW10 0SZ

■ @dinobooks
■ @footieheroesbks
www.heroesfootball.com
www.bonnierbooks.co.uk

Design and typesetting by www.envydesign.co.uk

Paperback ISBN: 978 1 78 606 808 8
E-book ISBN: 978 1 78606 890 3

British Library Cataloguing-in-Publication Data:
A catalogue record for this book is available from the British Library.

Printed and bound in Great Britain by Clays Ltd, Elcograf S.p.A.

9 10

Every attempt has been made to contact the relevant copyright-holders, but some
were unobtainable. We would be grateful if the appropriate people could contact us.

For Noah and Nico,
Southampton's future strikeforce

Matt Oldfield is an accomplished writer and the editor-in-chief
of football review site Of Pitch & Page. Tom Oldfield is a freelance
sports writer and the author of biographies on Cristiano Ronaldo,
Arsène Wenger and Rafael Nadal.

Cover illustration by Dan Leydon.
To learn more about Dan visit danleydon.com
To purchase his artwork visit etsy.com/shop/footynews
Or just follow him on Twitter @danleydon

TABLE OF CONTENTS

CHAPTER 1 – **CHELSEA ARE CHAMPIONS** 11

CHAPTER 2 – **A FOOTBALL FAMILY** 16

CHAPTER 3 – **PITCH INVADER** 22

CHAPTER 4 – **THE NEXT LEVEL** 27

CHAPTER 5 – **THE HAZARD BROTHERS** 32

CHAPTER 6 – **FRENCH FASCINATION** 37

CHAPTER 7 – **IMPRESSING A BELGIAN LEGEND** 43

CHAPTER 8 – **NATACHA** 48

CHAPTER 9 – **FOLLOWING IN THE FOOTSTEPS OF HEROES** . 54

CHAPTER 10 – **THE NEW MESSI** 59

CHAPTER 11 – **LEARNING LESSONS I** 67

CHAPTER 12 – **PIZZA AT PINO'S** 74

CHAPTER 13 – **YOUNG PLAYER OF THE YEAR** 80

CHAPTER 14 – **PRAISE FROM ZIDANE** 87

CHAPTER 15 – **LEARNING LESSONS II** 94

CHAPTER 16 – **TREBLE TIME** 99

CHAPTER 17 – **LAST SEASON AT LILLE** 106

CHAPTER 18 – **CHASED BY CHELSEA** 113

CHAPTER 19 – **WELCOME TO THE PREMIER LEAGUE** 120

CHAPTER 20 – **THE SPECIAL ONE** 128

CHAPTER 21 – **BELGIANS IN BRAZIL** 136

CHAPTER 22 – **EDEN'S BIG SEASON** 144

CHAPTER 23 – **PLAYER OF THE YEAR** 150

ACKNOWLEDGEMENTS

This was a very special opportunity for us, as brothers, to work together on something we are both so passionate about. Football has always been a big part of our lives. We hope this book will inspire others to start – or continue – playing football and chasing their dreams.

Writing a book like this was one of our dreams, and we are extremely thankful to John Blake Publishing and James Hodgkinson and Chris Mitchell, in particular, for making this project possible. It was great to have your guidance and support throughout our writing process.

We are also grateful to all the friends and family

that encouraged us along the way. Your interest and sense of humour helped to keep us on track. Will, Doug, Mills, John, James Pang-Oldfield and the rest of our King Edward VI friends, our aunts, uncles, cousins, the Nottingham and Montreal families and so many others – thank you all.

Melissa, we could not have done this without your understanding and support. Thank you for being as excited about this collaboration as we were. Iona, thank you for your kindness and encouragement during long, work-filled weekends.

Noah, we're doing our best to make football your favourite sport! We look forward to reading this book with you in the years ahead.

Mum and Dad, the biggest 'thank you' is reserved for you. You introduced us to football and then devoted hours and hours to taking us to games. You bought the tickets, the kits, the boots. We love football because you encouraged us to. Thank you for all the love, all the laughs and for always believing in us. This book is for you.

CHAPTER 1

CHELSEA ARE CHAMPIONS

Stamford Bridge, London, 3 May 2015

Eden, Eden, Eden, Eden, Eden, Eden...EDEN HAZARD!
Come on Chelsea!

At the end of the first half, Willian backheeled the ball and Eden ran into the box at speed. As usual, there were two players marking him and as he used his skills to try to get past them, they brought him down. As he lay on the floor, Eden looked up at the referee. Penalty!

Cesc Fàbregas helped him back to his feet, saying: 'When you run at defenders, there's nothing they can do except foul you!'

There was no doubt which Chelsea player would take the penalty. Eden was very proud of his 100 per cent scoring record and everyone expected him to make it 1– 0.

As he waited for the referee's whistle with his hands on his hips, he thought back to captain John Terry's pre-game message: 'If we win today, we win the Premier League title.' The crowd at Stamford Bridge was completely silent; everyone knew how important this goal could be. It was a good thing Eden didn't feel pressure.

The goalkeeper was moving around on his goal-line, trying to put him off. Eden stepped up and shot to the right but it wasn't as powerful as normal and it wasn't heading for the corner. The keeper saved it but the ball bounced out. Eden reacted first, beating the Crystal Palace defenders to head the ball into the net. Goooooooooooooooaaaaaaaaaaaaaaallllllllllllllllllllllll!

Eden wiped the sweat off his forehead. He hated missing penalties but at least he had scored the rebound. There was relief in the stands too; Chelsea were still on track to become champions. Nemanja

Matić lifted Eden into the air and Didier Drogba gave
him a big hug.

'We can talk about that awful penalty later,' he
joked. 'Right now, we're forty-five minutes away
from the Premier League title!'

At the final whistle, everyone celebrated. Chelsea
manager José Mourinho congratulated his coaches
on the touchline, owner Roman Abramovich punched
the air with joy and the players hugged each other
and formed a big circle. Eden was their star but
the entire team had all played really well for the
whole season.

'We've done it!' Eden shouted to Cesc. 'We're
champions!'

Wearing Chelsea caps and scarves, they ran to the
fans and clapped every single one of them for all of
their support. Eden loved to entertain them and they
loved him for that. The fans never stopped singing:

Blue is the colour, football is the game,
We're all together and winning is our aim.

Captain John Terry ran to Eden and gave him a
massive hug.

'What a season!' he laughed. 'Luckily we had the best player in the league in our team!'

It was the happiest moment of Eden's life. Winning the French league with Lille had been great but the Premiership was the best league in the world.

Eden found his wife Natacha and kissed her. His family meant the world to him and he was so glad that they could share his joy. He took his sons out on to the pitch in their Chelsea shirts with their names on the back and Eden's Number 10. Holding Yannis's hand and with Leo in his arms, he walked around the pitch with the fans cheering his name. It was a moment that Eden would never forget.

When they spotted Eden's parents and brothers in the crowd, they waved. Growing up in a football-mad family had been the perfect place to start and he was very grateful for their support over the years.

There was one last person that Eden needed to thank.

'You've taught me so much,' he said to Mourinho, 'and now I'm playing the best football of my life.'

'That's not because of me,' Mourinho replied

modestly. 'That's because of you and your hard work. Congratulations and enjoy yourself!'

He was right – Eden had worked very hard to prove his critics wrong and become a team leader. His skills had always been incredible but Eden now had new sides to his game – strength, determination and consistency. The supporters could rely on his moments of magic in almost every match.

It had been an amazing and sometimes difficult journey from the back garden in Belgium to Europe's top young talent and now to Premier League champion and Player of the Year. Eden had enjoyed every minute of it and he couldn't wait to see what he would achieve next.

CHAPTER 2

A FOOTBALL FAMILY

'Eden! Eden!' Grandma Nicole shouted happily
from the house. Grandpa Francis was playing
football with his grandson in the garden. Eden was
only two years old but he could already kick the
ball hard. He couldn't really aim his shot, though,
and so his grandpa had to keep getting the ball out
of the flowerbeds.

Grandma Nicole had just got off the phone with
Eden's father, Thierry. 'Eden, come on, we've got
to go to the hospital. It's time to meet your new
brother!'

Eden wasn't sure about having a brother. Until
now he had been the star of the show and got lots

of attention from his parents and grandparents. But now they would have to look after the new baby and they might not have time to play football with him. Eden sat down in the grass and refused to move.

'Aren't you excited to see him?' Grandpa Francis asked, picking him up and taking him inside to get ready.

'No!' he replied, shaking his head violently.

In the hospital, Eden's dad proudly showed him the baby – he couldn't believe how tiny it was.

'Eden, this is your brother, Thorgan,' Thierry said. 'Isn't he lovely? A couple of years ago, you were that small too!'

Carine could see that her older son wasn't happy about the new arrival. 'Don't look so sad – soon you'll be able to play football together.'

'One more child and you'll have a great five-a-side team!' Grandpa Francis joked.

Football was the Hazard family passion. Thierry and Carine had both been professional footballers. Thierry had played for the Belgian national team and Carine had only stopped playing when she was pregnant with Eden. There were footballs all over the house and they lived right next to the ground of R.A.A. Louviéroise, the third division team that Thierry still played for. So it was lucky that Eden seemed to love football just as much as his parents did.

'Eden, would you like to go and see your dad play today?' Carine asked, as she made him breakfast. He was now nearly four and old enough to sit in the stands.

'Yes!' Eden shouted straight away. He had been waiting for this day for months. He already had his own green-and-white team shirt with 'Hazard' on the back. He couldn't wait to wear it.

'Okay, Grandma Nicole will look after Thorgan,' Carine said. 'And we'll go and cheer Daddy on!'

From their garden, they could always hear the crowd on match days but being inside the *Stade du Tivoli* was so much better. It wasn't a big stadium but 13,000 people could make plenty of noise. Once,

Thierry had taken Eden out on to the pitch after a match to kick a ball around. To the youngster, it felt like the biggest pitch in the world.

'Eden, can you see Daddy?' Carine asked as they watched the team warming up. She lifted him up onto the seat so that he got a better view. He was wearing the full La Louvière kit: shirt, shorts and socks. Eden had tried to wear his little football boots with studs too but Carine had stopped him.

'Yes, there he is!' he replied, pointing out onto the pitch. 'Daddy!' he shouted and Thierry turned and waved at them. Eden felt really proud that his dad was one of the star players.

Throughout the match, Eden watched his dad carefully. He wasn't the quickest player but he was calm on the ball and he gave good passes to his teammates. He also made some really good tackles.

'Why doesn't Daddy shoot?' Eden asked at half-time.

'Daddy isn't a striker, darling. I was a striker and I scored lots of goals,' Carine replied with a laugh.

'Daddy defends the goal and tries to set up goals for the strikers.'

'When can I watch you play, Mummy?' was Eden's next question. 'I like goals!'

'Sorry, I don't play football anymore,' Carine said, ruffling his hair. 'But you were in my stomach for three months when I was still playing. You helped me score lots of goals. Now I don't have time with you two rascals to look after!'

Eden loved his first football match. La Louvière didn't win but Thierry played well and after the final whistle, he came up into the crowd to say hello.

'Did you enjoy that?' he asked. He was sweaty and out of breath. He had mud all over his shirt and his knees too.

'Yes!' Eden shouted with a huge smile on his face.

'Would you like to come out on the pitch with me? I need to thank the supporters and you could come and clap with me.'

Eden eagerly followed his dad and waved and clapped for the fans. They cheered back at him and he felt like a hero. It was the happiest day of his young life.

'One day, I'm going to play football for a big team like you!' he told Thierry as they went into the dressing room. All of the players said hello to him and so did the manager. Eden felt like one of the team.

'If you work hard, you could play for an even bigger club than this,' his dad told him.

Eden loved that idea. He wanted to play in front of millions of fans and score lots and lots of goals. He wanted to be the best player in the world. He couldn't wait to get back into the garden to practise.

CHAPTER 3

PITCH INVADER

As Pascal Delmoitiez looked out on the Royal Stade Brainois pitch, he could see that there was someone playing on it. 'Not again,' the caretaker said to himself as he started walking from the clubhouse towards the other end to deal with the problem. He wasn't happy. The pitch had just been reseeded and the grass needed time to grow. No-one was ever allowed to play on it between matches but this week that was particularly important.

Avenue du Stade wasn't the biggest football stadium but Pascal was very proud of it. Royal Stade Brainois played in the fifth division of the Belgian league and the club only had one stand for their small group of supporters. On the other three sides of the pitch, grassy banks made it feel very different to massive city stadiums. The quality of football might not have been the best, but rules were rules and this kid was in trouble.

As he got past the halfway line, Pascal saw that it wasn't one of the local teenagers who often jumped the fence to practise late at night. That was a relief because it was often hard to get rid of them. This boy was much smaller than that; he couldn't have been more than six years old. He placed the ball on the penalty spot and, with a short run-up, kicked it into the top corner. Then he collected the ball from the goal, and repeated the exercise again and again.

'Wow, how does he get so much power on his shot?' the caretaker thought to himself. He wasn't angry anymore; he was amazed. He was watching pure natural talent. Most kids that young could barely reach the goal from twelve yards with a plastic football, let alone a full-size leather one. And the boy wasn't even wearing any shoes or socks.

Pascal was getting close now. Suddenly the boy

realised that he'd been caught. In a flash, he picked up the ball and ran behind the goal as fast as he could. By the corner flag, he jumped the low fence back into his garden. The caretaker knew exactly whose home that was. He decided to go and knock on the front door.

'Pascal, how are you?' Thierry said when he answered. 'What can I do for you?'

'I just went to check on the new pitch and I found someone playing on it. When he saw me, he escaped into your back garden. Who do you think it could have been?' the caretaker asked with a smile on his face.

'Eden!' Thierry shouted straight away. After a few moments, his son came running in. His feet were covered in mud and guilt was written all over his little face.

'Where have you been?' his dad asked him calmly.

'Nowhere, I was just playing football in the garden,' Eden said quickly, looking down at the floor.

'That's interesting,' Thierry said, giving the caretaker a wink. 'Pascal says he found a troublemaker messing up the new pitch. And he says the troublemaker escaped into our garden. Did you see anyone else out there?'

Eden couldn't lie anymore; he'd been caught and he didn't want to make things any worse than they already were. 'I'm sorry!' he said. He hated being told off.

'Son, how many times have I told you that you can't play out there? The pitch needs to be kept in good condition for the league matches. Your mum and I will need to come up with a punishment for you,' Thierry replied, putting on his 'serious father' face. 'Now go to your room while I sort things out with Pascal.'

Eden walked slowly up the stairs, leaving dirty footprints on each step. He was worried about what his mum would say – this wasn't the first time that he had got himself into trouble. When he did something naughty, his parents usually told him no football for a week – no playing it and no watching it on TV. That was the worst thing in the world. Life was so boring without football. Plus, he needed to practise every day if he wanted to be as good as his dad.

'I'm really sorry about that,' Thierry told the caretaker. 'It won't happen again, I promise. That boy just loves football so much – you can't stop him.'

'That's okay, I'll let him off this time. You should have seen him, though – he's barely higher than the grass and he was kicking it harder than some of our senior players! You've got a really good player there. How old is he?'

'Five. Yes, he'll be better than me in no time!'

'I suppose the son of two footballers has a pretty good chance of being a special player. Do you think he'd like to come and train with our juniors?' Pascal asked. They were always looking for new local players and Eden seemed perfect even if he was a bit young.

'I'm sure he'd love to but that isn't much of a punishment, is it?' Thierry laughed.

CHAPTER 4

THE NEXT LEVEL

Eden loved playing for the Royal Stade Brainois juniors. He was their star player – the best passer, the best dribbler and the top goal-scorer by miles. The coach had given up on trying to teach Eden new tactics. He was a natural talent and he was teaching himself all the time. Even at the age of eight, he was already determined to be the best at everything.

'Come on, we need to go home!' Thierry shouted from the touchline. The training session had ended twenty minutes earlier but his son was still out on the pitch working on his skills. Thierry was hungry and he had Thorgan and now Kylian to look after too. The Hazard family five-a-side team was complete.

'One minute, Dad!' he replied. 'I'm learning a new
trick and I've nearly got it.'

At school and at home, it was very difficult to get
Eden to concentrate on anything for longer than a
few minutes. But with a ball at his feet, he would
spend hours doing the same skill over and over again
until it was perfect. 'If only every maths problem was
about football!' Thierry thought to himself.

Word was already spreading about Eden's
wizardry. Fathi Ennabli was the youth co-ordinator at
A.F.C. Tubize, a Belgian Second Division team based
just five kilometres away. Fathi was spending more
time at Royal Stade Brainois than he was at his own
club, and he was desperate to sign Eden.

'I've never seen a youngster that comes close to
him,' he told the Tubize youth team coaches with
great excitement. 'We need him!'

Fathi had first seen Eden in a local youth
tournament. It took a lot to catch his eye at one of
these big events but this tiny kid was out of this
world. Every time he got the ball, something special
happened. His control was perfect and with a nice

burst of speed, he glided past players as if they weren't even there. He was a little selfish with the ball sometimes but that was something you could work on. And if you were that much better than everyone else, why would you pass?

'Who's that? He's incredible!' Fathi asked one of the Brainois coaches on the touchline.

'Eden Hazard,' he replied in a tone that suggested he'd had to answer that question many times. 'Mark my words – that kid's going to be the future of Belgium.'

After that, Fathi went to every Brainois youth game and stood next to more and more scouts from other teams. It was a competition now and there was no way he was going to lose. He introduced himself to Thierry.

'Very nice to meet you,' Fathi said, shaking hands. He meant business. 'Your son is a fantastic talent and I won't stop until I sign him for Tubize.'

Thierry laughed; this wasn't the first youth scout to say that and it definitely wouldn't be the last. 'Thanks but he's not going anywhere right now – he enjoys it here and this is home. I'm sorry, he's not ready for the step-up just yet.'

'I understand,' Fathi replied. 'We'll keep watching Eden and when you feel he's ready for a new challenge, let me know. Tubize is a really friendly club and it's just up the road!'

'It's a very good offer and we'll certainly consider it,' Thierry replied politely. There was no way that he would make a decision without listening to Eden first.

He knew that his son was good enough to play for a bigger club but he wanted to protect him as much as possible. Football academies could be very tough places and he wanted to make sure that his son could handle the physical and emotional pressure.

'Son, are you happy at Brainois?' Thierry asked him at dinner one night. He had noticed that he wasn't playing with quite the same passion in recent matches.

Eden thought for a moment. 'I have lots of friends here but I'm a bit bored, Dad. I think I'm ready to play at a higher level.'

Thierry nodded – it was time. He kept to his word and when Eden turned ten, he joined his dad at A.F.C. Tubize. After two years of fighting, Fathi finally had his player.

'This is the best day of my career!' he told Thierry when he brought Eden along for his first training session. 'Once I knew Anderlecht and Standard Liège had showed an interest, I didn't think we had a chance.'

'My wife and I talked about it and we decided that Eden needs to stay close to home for now,' Thierry replied. 'I know you'll look after him here and really help him to develop as a player. And I also love the idea of father and son playing for the same team!'

Thierry hugged his son but Eden wasn't listening. He was too busy watching the football being played on the pitch behind. This was the next level and he couldn't wait.

CHAPTER 5

THE HAZARD BROTHERS

'How was it?' Thorgan asked excitedly when Eden got home from that first practice at Tubize. He was only two years younger and he wanted to copy everything his older brother did, including his ambition to become a great footballer. He had been watching the road, waiting for their car to return.

'It was amazing!' Eden replied with a big smile that wouldn't leave his face for hours. 'There are some really good players but I think I did well.'

The other kids had been nice but Eden felt it would take a bit of time to break into the gang. Most of them had been playing together for years and knew each other really well. They had their own jokes and on the pitch they had that silent understanding that Eden and Thorgan had as brothers. He hoped that his talent would help him to win friends.

The Tubize training field was bigger than the one at Brainois and the surface was much nicer. The ball moved quickly but Eden soon got used to it. Everyone had yellow club kits and he loved feeling like a professional footballer. If he kept doing well, maybe he would get to play with his dad in the senior team one day.

In the training exercises, Eden had lots of chances to impress with his control, dribbling and passing. Thierry stayed to watch but he hid by the corner flag so that he didn't put his son off. Fathi was also there but he stood on the touchline and shouted encouragement. He was very proud of his new signing.

'Nice touch, Eden!'

'That's it, look up and play the ball into Daniel's feet. Lovely!'

In the match at the end, Eden worked hard to get the ball as often as he could. 'Don't try to be too clever', he told himself whenever he thought about dribbling around defenders. He didn't want to be the new boy who turned up and just showed off.

At Brainois, Eden had been average height but at Tubize he was definitely one of the smallest. The boys were also much stronger than at his former club, and Eden would need to get better at dealing with more physical tackles from defenders. At least his judo training was proving useful; it kept him light on his feet and it meant he knew how to fall without hurting himself. Eden was exhausted but happy with the start he had made. And he had lots more to offer next time.

'Did you do all of your tricks?' Kylian asked. He was six now and there was always a football glued to his foot. Thorgan was helping him with his skills every day and he was determined to follow in his elder brothers' footsteps.

'No, I kept it pretty simple today. But don't worry, I'll soon show them what I can do!'

The Hazard brothers often talked about how good it would be when they all played in the same team, destroying the opposition together. Opponents wouldn't know what to do with the three of them attacking as a unit.

'Dinner time!' Carine shouted. Thorgan and Kylian rushed to help set the table. Once Eden could smell the food, he too got up off the sofa. It was spaghetti bolognese, the family favourite.

'Mum, when can I join Tubize?' Thorgan asked with his mouth full. He was eight and scouts were starting to turn up to his Brainois games too. 'The next Hazard' they called him. It would be hard to keep him quiet now that his brother had joined a bigger club.

'When you learn to eat properly – that's disgusting!' Carine laughed. Unfortunately, her sons weren't such quick learners when it came to table manners.

'Eden, you were great today. How are you feeling?' Thierry asked. He was really glad that his son had enjoyed the new experience. They didn't want to push their children into playing football – they would support them in whatever they wanted to do.

'I'm pretty tired now,' Eden said as he served himself seconds. Football was hungry work and he was a growing boy. He needed to be a few inches taller to play at this higher level.

'But you'll come out and play with us in the garden for a bit?' Kylian asked, worried that their routine might be changing. He had lots of practice to do and he needed his brother's help. They had about an hour until it would get too dark to see the ball.

'Of course!' Eden replied, wolfing down the last of his dinner.

CHAPTER 6

FRENCH FASCINATION

'Eden, it's starting!' Kylian shouted, and his older brother came running into the living room to join the rest of the family. Their favourite TV show was about to begin and there was no way Eden ever missed it. *Téléfoot* was a weekly programme like *Match of the Day* that showed the highlights from the weekend's French league games. The Hazard brothers loved the top goalscorers Didier Drogba and Djibril Cissé and the clever playmakers like Juninho Pernambucano and Ronaldinho. Tonight's programme was a special one.

'I can't wait to see Ronaldinho's goal!' Thorgan said with excitement.

'They're already calling it goal of the season,' Thierry added.

When *Téléfoot* was on, Eden stayed silent. He didn't take notes on paper but in his head, he recorded every bit of skill that he saw. Then he spent hours in the garden and on the training pitch making sure that he could do them perfectly.

The Guingamp vs Paris Saint-Germain match was up first. Ronaldinho got the ball on the left just inside the opposition half. He ran forward and then played a neat one-two. As the ball came back to him, a defender dived in for a tackle but Ronaldinho flicked it beautifully over him. With the ball at his feet, he ran towards the box, moving one way and then the other at high speed. In the penalty area, another defender came across but with an amazing stepover, Ronaldinho dribbled right past him. He only had the goalkeeper to beat and he chipped the ball over him and into the net.

'Wow!' Kylian shouted.

'That's incredible!' Carine agreed.

'How does he do that?' Thorgan asked but he didn't expect an answer. It was magic.

Eden was still quiet; he wanted to see it again. Ronaldinho's feet moved so quickly and he had perfect balance when he ran with the ball. It often looked like he was dancing. It was dark outside but he was desperate to go and copy the Brazilian's moves.

'Give me a couple of hours and I'll be able to do that,' he told his family, with a very serious look on his face. Carine sighed; her son never stopped.

Eden's favourite footballer, however, was a Frenchman playing in Spain – Real Madrid's Zinedine Zidane. He had never seen anyone like him – he was strong, calm and played the best passes in the world. He could watch videos of '*Zizou*' for hours and sometimes they showed France national team matches on TV in Belgium. They had been terrible in the World Cup tournament of 2002, but Zidane was still his hero.

Whenever he could, Eden liked to play the

'*Zizou*' role for Tubize – in front of the midfield
but behind the striker. As a 'Number 10', he had
the freedom and space to use his tricks to create
goals and score some too. It was the position
everyone wanted to play but Eden was full of
self-belief.

'I'm good and I know I am!' he told his
teammates and they trusted him to win games for
them. It wasn't quite a one-boy team but Eden
was certainly the star. He was playing against
older and bigger boys but he was totally fearless.
In one match, Tubize got a free-kick a few metres
outside the penalty area. There was no question
of who would take it. Eden stepped up and
curled it around the wall and into the top corner.
Goooooaaaaaaaaaallllllllllll!

As the other players ran to celebrate with him, the
referee stopped them.

'No goal!' he shouted. 'I hadn't blown the whistle,
so you need to take it again.'

Everyone else was really disappointed but Eden
didn't mind. He put the ball down, took a deep

breath and waited for the whistle. Like *Zizou*, he was always cool and focused.

'I'd like to see him do that again,' Thierry said with a smile. As ever, he was on the touchline watching his son and challenging him to be the best.

Eden curled the ball into the same corner again, and this time it was a goal. He made it look so easy.

The players were all amazed but Thierry just laughed. 'I think he heard me and did that to annoy me!'

There was nothing Eden couldn't do with the ball at his feet. Opponents kicked and pushed him but he was too good to be stopped. Word was already spreading across Belgium and even into France about his talent. Everything was going according to plan.

'When I'm older, I want to play in the French league,' he told his brothers as they played together in the garden. Thorgan had just moved from Brainois to Tubize like Eden, while Kylian had gone straight to Tubize. Where one brother went, the others soon followed.

'You'll be the new Thierry Henry!' Kylian said. He had total faith in his eldest brother's ability.

'No, the new Zidane!' Eden replied very quickly.

CHAPTER 7

IMPRESSING A BELGIAN LEGEND

Just as Eden was getting better and better, a footballing legend became a coach at Tubize. The timing was perfect. Enzo Scifo had been the captain of Belgium for many years and he played at four World Cups. He was a central midfielder and a very good passer who played for big club teams in Italy and France as well as Belgium. The player they used to call 'the Little Pele' could teach Eden lots of useful things.

'Has he been to watch you play yet?' Thorgan asked. Everyone at Tubize was waiting for their local hero to arrive. The youngsters were desperate to impress him.

'No, not yet but they say he's leading our session next week!' Eden replied. He couldn't wait to show off his talent.

Enzo was actually quite nervous when he turned up for his first practice. He hadn't been coaching for long and the kids would have had high expectations. He was still Belgium's most famous footballer, even though he was retired. He didn't want to disappoint them but he was still learning his new role. Hopefully they would be very good players and he could help them to improve.

'Hello, nice to meet you all. I'm Enzo Scifo,' he began. The players were standing around him, listening carefully to his every word. Today, no-one was messing around.

'We all know who you are!' one of the kids joked and everyone laughed.

'Yes, I guess you do!' Enzo replied, a little embarrassed. 'I'm really looking forward to working with you all. This afternoon, we'll be doing lots of exercises to practise your technique because technique is always the most important thing. I wasn't the quickest footballer but I could pass the ball pretty well!'

Eden was very happy to hear that – he was really proud of his technique. Other players were taller and stronger but he definitely had the best skills in the Tubize youth team. 'This is your time to shine,' Eden told himself with a ball at his feet. He was full of confidence.

The boys were split up into small groups and Enzo walked around, watching and giving bits of advice. Every now and again, he would step in and show them how to do something. Enzo was too old to play professionally but he was still an excellent footballer. There were no weak players but he wasn't just looking for good – he was looking for great.

In the final group, at last he saw something really special. A small kid dribbled through a line of cones, the ball glued to his foot. Most players hit at least one cone along the way – but not this boy. Not only did he do it perfectly but he also did it at great speed. At the end of the cones, he played a good pass for the one-two and kept running. When the ball came back to him, the boy took a nice first touch, looked up and hit a powerful shot into the corner of the goal.

'Brilliant!' Enzo shouted, clapping loudly. 'What's your name?' he asked the boy.

'Eden,' the boy replied. 'Eden Hazard.'

'Well done, Eden. I don't think I've ever seen anyone do that so well, not even Thierry Henry!'

Nothing could have made Eden happier. Henry was another one of his heroes and Enzo had played with him at French club Monaco. It was such an honour to be compared to an international superstar. What a day it was turning out to be. Thorgan and Kylian would be so jealous when they heard about it.

In the match at the end of the session, Eden was everywhere and Enzo couldn't believe what he was seeing. This fourteen-year-old boy was so calm and clever on the ball and he was a lot stronger than he looked too. He could play with both feet and he could score goals. He needed to become more of a team player but that was easy to teach. It was a long time since Enzo had seen such a talented youngster.

'How did it go?' Leo, the regular coach, asked him afterwards as they put the balls, cones and bibs away.

'It was good,' Enzo replied. 'No, it was better than that – it was brilliant!'

'I'm glad to hear that,' the coach said. He had been worried that Enzo would find it boring working with the youth team. 'Why was it so great?'

'I saw a very special player – a true phenomenon.'

'Let me guess – Eden?' Leo knew exactly who his best player was. It didn't take a genius to work that out.

'That's right – he's got an amazing future ahead of him,' Enzo said with a big smile on his face. 'We're very lucky to have him here at Tubize.'

'I know, I just hope we can hold on to him.'

CHAPTER 8

NATACHA

'Enzo said that I was better than Henry!' Eden boasted when he got home. He was twisting the truth a little but he didn't care. It was the best day of his life and he wanted to tell the world about it.

'Wow! That's amazing,' Kylian said, giving him a high-five. He was very pleased for his brother and not at all surprised. He had no doubt that Eden was going to be a superstar.

'What else did he say?' Thorgan asked. He wanted to know everything about the training session. He was hoping that Enzo would come and coach the Under-12s too one day.

'He said that if I kept working hard, I would be a great player,' Eden said, throwing himself down on the sofa. 'What a day!' He was tired but very, very happy. He would never forget Enzo's words.

Football was the main thing in Eden's life but he had also met a girl that he really liked. Natacha went to the same school and he finally plucked up the courage to ask her out on a date to the cinema. She was very beautiful, kind and funny. She was close to her family too and he liked that about her. They got on really well, and she even played football.

'Did you kiss her?' Thorgan asked when Eden got home.

'I'm not telling you – leave me alone!' he said, going red. He was embarrassed and didn't want to share everything with his brothers. He was a teenager now, after all.

'What did you talk about – football?' Kylian asked. He rarely heard his brother talk about anything else.

'Only some of the time! We have lots of other things in common as well – music, food, films, TV shows.' Eden enjoyed the chance to talk about other subjects. It made a nice change from his football-mad family.

'When I saw you playing with the boys in the playground, I thought you were really arrogant,' Natacha had admitted to him as they waited for the film to start. 'But when you don't have a ball at your feet, you're actually really nice!'

'I know, I'm a very different person when I'm on the pitch,' Eden replied. 'Sorry about that but I'm very competitive and I always want to win.'

'That's okay, as long as you're like this when you're off it,' Natacha had said, giving his hand a squeeze. Eden was very pleased with how it was going. He was too shy to kiss her on their first date but there was plenty of time for that.

'Do you ask her for another date?' Thorgan wanted to know. 'She's really pretty!'

'Stop asking so many questions!' Eden replied. He much preferred talking about football with his brothers. 'Yes, we're going to town next weekend.'

'In the afternoon, I hope,' Carine said from

the kitchen. She'd been listening to the whole conversation, and was pleased that her son had a new interest beyond football. 'You're too young to go out at night!'

'Mum, mind your own business!' Eden said, going off to his bedroom.

At Tubize, he was also getting lots of attention. Every time he played, there was a group of scouts on the touchline, some from top Belgian clubs but some from France and other European countries.

'Eden, your fan club is here again,' his teammates would joke before kick-off. By now, they were used to crowds of people watching their star player. 'Give them a wave!'

Eden loved playing for Tubize but he was starting to think about the next step. He wanted to compete at the top level against the best young players around. Eden knew that the top Belgian team, Anderlecht, were interested but French club Lille were also asking about him all the time. They were one of the best teams in Ligue 1 and they were only half an hour away by train.

'Lille is a very good club and their academy has a great reputation for getting the best out of young players,' Thierry said over dinner one night. He knew it was important to keep giving his son new challenges and he could see that he was getting a bit restless.

'And it's not far away – you could still live at home,' Kylian added. He wasn't ready for his brother to move away. He still had so much to learn from him.

'No son, I'm afraid they have a boarding school at Lille,' Carine replied. 'Eden would go to live there but he would come back for the holidays, I promise.'

The Hazard brothers looked at each other – it was a big step for Eden to go and live in France without them. But at the same time, it was exactly what he needed to continue his development.

'At the academy, they play football all day every day,' Eden told Thorgan excitedly. 'There's a bit of school work but not much.'

'That sounds amazing!' Thorgan replied. He was

very jealous but he hoped to follow him to France as
soon as possible.

CHAPTER 9

FOLLOWING IN THE FOOTSTEPS OF HEROES

'We've found this incredible kid playing for the
A.F.C. Tubize youth team,' the Lille OSC scouts had
told Jean-Michel Vandamme, the academy director,
after a trip to a youth tournament in Brussels. 'His
name is Eden Hazard. You'll want to come and have
a look at him.'

Jean-Michel trusted his scouts and so he
soon came to watch Eden play. Standing on the
touchline before the game, he recognised several
scouts from other top European clubs. 'This kid is
clearly a big deal,' Jean-Michel thought to himself.
He loved the feeling of discovering great young
talent – he still remembered the first time he had

seen French international Franck Ribéry playing
in Boulogne.

His first thought about Eden was that he was
very skinny. Taking up his position for kick-off, the
kid looked a lot smaller than almost every other
player on the pitch. It was a common problem
with very talented players – could they deal with
big, tough-tackling defenders? Strength could be
built up, however. The most important thing was
natural skill. If he didn't have that then there was
no chance.

It quickly became clear that Eden had lots and
lots of natural skill. He moved around the pitch
with such confidence and you could tell that he
was thinking more quickly than anyone else. 'Very
fast football brain,' Jean-Michel wrote down in his
notebook. Everything the youngster did was very
impressive – this was a high quality player that Lille
definitely wanted to sign.

'Hello, Thierry, isn't it?' he said, shaking Eden's
father's hand. He had done his homework on
the family. 'Nice to meet you, I'm Jean-Michel

Vandamme and I run the football academy at Lille. Your son is a very talented footballer.'

'Thank you,' Thierry replied politely. He was very used to these meetings by now. 'Yes, Eden is doing very well.'

'We'd love for him to join our club,' Jean-Michel continued. 'As you know, our academy is very strong and we really look after our young players. Eden will need to join a bigger club soon and we'd really like you to think about Lille.'

'Yes, we will certainly think about it,' Thierry told him but he wouldn't say any more. They were determined to let Eden make his own decision about what team he played for next.

Nearly eighteen months passed, and after lots more matches and lots more long conversations, Eden was finally about to sign for Lille. Jean-Michel was pleased that all of his hard work had paid off. They now had one of the best young players he had ever seen. Tubize were sad to see Eden leave but they had known for a long time that it was coming. They understood that it was time for him to move on to bigger and better things.

'Remember us when you win the French title!' Fathi laughed as they said their goodbyes. Eden was very grateful for everything that the club had done for him. It would always have a special place in his heart.

The whole Hazard family travelled to France for Eden to sign his Lille contract. Jean-Michel greeted them and gave them a full tour of the football facilities and the boarding school where Eden would be staying with his new teammates.

'Wow, can I sign too?' Kylian said as he looked at all of the perfect football pitches and the big changing rooms.

'Yes, we'll offer you a deal for all three of us!' Thorgan added and everyone laughed. Eden would certainly miss his brothers.

After a delicious lunch, Jean-Michel took Eden and Thierry into his office. 'So, did you like what you saw this morning?' he asked them. On the walls, he had pictures of Ribéry and other top players that he had worked with over the years. Eden was clearly in very safe hands here at Lille.

'Yes thanks, I think I'll be very happy here,' he replied. Everything felt very big and professional but he knew he would quickly get used to that. He was excited to get started on the football field and show the coaches and players just what he could do. He would let his football do the talking.

'Great, we're really looking forward to having you here,' Jean-Michel said, putting the contract in front of him. 'We have high hopes for you!'

Eden picked up a pen and signed the contract. He had high hopes for himself too. 'When I'm sixteen, I'm going to be in the first team,' he said, laying out his career plans. 'I want to play in front of massive crowds and entertain them with my skills.' Jean-Michel wasn't sure whether to laugh but Eden and Thierry both looked serious. It was a crazy aim but he had never seen such bold ambition in a player so young. He had a feeling that they had some great years ahead of them.

CHAPTER 10

THE NEW MESSI

After the first few weeks, Eden started to really enjoy the Lille boarding school. He did miss home and Natacha but it was fun living with his teammates and he soon had lots of friends.

'Shall we go and have a quick kick-a-round after dinner?' Jérémy asked. For Eden, it was just like being back at home with Thorgan and Kylian.

On the pitch, things were also going well. Eden settled in quickly and his coaches were impressed. Stéphane Adam had heard lots about him from Jean-Michel and the club scouts. He was looking forward to seeing just how good Eden really was.

'Everyone, please give a warm welcome to

Eden,' Stéphane told the players at the first training session. 'He's joined us from Tubize in Belgium.'

Eden didn't say a lot but it was clear that he had plenty of self-confidence. As he got involved in the exercises, he didn't look at all nervous. In fact, he came alive with the ball at his feet.

'That's it, Eden – very nice!' Stéphane shouted out as he saw the youth control the ball perfectly and play a great cross-field pass.

It was very early days but he reminded Stéphane of the best player in the world, Barcelona's Lionel Messi. Like Messi, Eden wasn't very big but he had the skill, balance and pace to get away from defenders in really small spaces. It was so exciting to watch. He didn't want to put too much pressure on the kid but he knew that he was good enough to reach the very top.

It was a real pleasure to work with such a rare talent. Sometimes he needed to be told to work harder for the team but most of the time, if you got the ball to Eden he would do something special. He won game after game for the Under-16s with his quick thinking and skill.

'Eden to the rescue again!' his teammate Omar joked. His killer pass had set up another winning goal.

Eden could feel himself getting better and better every day at Lille. 'It's football 24-7 here,' he told Thorgan on the phone. 'You'd love it here. There are some really great players in my team but you know me, I'm determined to be the best.'

By May 2007, Eden was back in Tubize. This time, however, he was playing for the Belgium Under-17s at the European Championships. It was really nice to be back in town.

'This is home for me!' he told his teammate Christian Benteke as they arrived at the stadium for their tough opening match against the Netherlands. 'The pressure's on for me to play well.'

With the match tied at 1–1, Eden was fouled and won a penalty. He picked himself up and scored it. It was a great feeling to score at *Stade Leburton* with so many friends and family cheering him on in the stands.

In the semi-finals, Belgium played Spain and they were winning with twenty minutes to go, thanks to Eden. Nill De Pauw played a great ball to him and from a tight angle, his powerful shot hit a defender and went into the net.

'Come on, let's hold on for the win!' Eden shouted to his teammates as they celebrated. He had quickly become one of the team leaders.

Sadly, Spain scored and the match went to penalties. With Christian off the field, Eden knew he had to take one. 'I'll go fourth,' he told the coach, Bob Browaeys. He scored but they lost 7– 6. It was a horrible way to go out of the tournament but they had done very well to get so far.

'Great game,' Browaeys said, putting an arm around Eden's shoulder. He was sitting on his own on the pitch. 'You didn't deserve to be on the losing side. Don't worry, you've got a great future ahead of you.'

It was nice to hear but it didn't make the defeat any easier. In the dressing room, the players were sitting in silence with their heads in their hands.

Eden tried to raise their spirits, saying: 'We have a really good team and this was just the warm-up for the World Cup!'

The Under-17 World Cup took place in South Korea just a few months later. Eden was really excited to travel with his teammates and play in a huge international tournament. All of the big clubs would be watching and looking for the next superstar. In 2003, Cesc Fàbregas and David Silva had been the stars and now they played in the Champions League. If he did well, Eden could be next.

'This is an amazing opportunity for us,' Christian said as they walked around the city of Changwon, taking in the great atmosphere. 'We can win this!'

Eden smiled and nodded. Hopes were high amongst the Belgium squad before the tournament but sadly it was a total disaster. Eden played every minute of the three group matches but he couldn't score or save his team from defeat.

'I can't believe it,' he told Christian once the disappointment had faded a little. He hated losing more than anything. 'I really thought we would at least reach the semi-finals.'

'I know but we just didn't play well enough,' his teammate replied. 'We must do better next time.'

Eden had learnt a lot from the painful experience and he returned to Lille determined to move onwards and upwards. His great performances for the Under-18s team soon impressed the senior team manager, Claude Puel. He wanted 'Little Messi' in the first team as quickly as possible.

'Congratulations, you're moving up to the reserves for this season,' Stéphane told Eden after training one day. He was sorry to be losing such a great talent but he knew Eden was ready for a new challenge. He would still play for the youth team too but Eden was so pleased to be moving towards the senior squad. He was only sixteen so his target was still possible.

'That's great news!' Thierry said when he heard the news. He had real faith in all of his sons. 'You'll be getting your full debut soon.'

That came sooner than anyone expected. In November 2007, Lille had a friendly against Belgian side Club Brugge. A lot of their stars were away playing for their countries and so Claude Puel needed players.

'It's a good chance to give some of the youth players some match experience. Let's call up Hazard,' Puel told his coaching staff.

With his whole family in the stands watching, Eden started the match on the bench.

'Surely they'll bring him on soon!' Kylian said with twenty minutes of the game left to go. He was so excited to see his brother out on the field.

He was right. Eden had been warming up along the touchline for five minutes when one of the coaches called him back. 'You're going on,' he told him.

Eden did his final stretches and ran on to the pitch. It was a great feeling to wear the white-and-red Lille shirt in a senior match. He ran and ran until the final whistle, getting on the ball as much as possible. Eden was sad when it was over but he hoped he had done enough to make the squad again.

'Well done,' Claude Puel said, patting him on the

back. 'You caused them lots of problems when you came on. You looked a natural out there!'

Eden couldn't stop smiling. He went out for dinner with his family afterwards but all he could think about were the manager's words.

'What was it like?' Thorgan asked. He had just joined another French club, Lens, and he dreamt of making his debut.

'Amazing!' was all Eden could say.

The next day he was back training with the reserves but he would spend the week waiting to see if he would be picked for the next Ligue 1 game against Nancy. Had he done enough in the friendly?

CHAPTER 11

LEARNING LESSONS I

'I think you've got a good chance of being on the bench at least,' Omar told Eden as they passed the ball between them before training. 'Puel likes young players and you're the best around!'

'I hope you're right,' Eden replied. Patience wasn't one of his strengths. He knew he was still very young but he couldn't wait to play at the top level. He knew he was good enough.

Finally, he was selected as a substitute for the game against Nancy and with fifteen minutes of the match to go, he made his debut. He was still sixteen – he had achieved his aim with two whole months to spare. 'I told you, Jean-Michel!' he said to himself as he got ready to go on. It was an incredible moment to run on to the field in front of 20,000 fans. That was what he'd been dreaming of ever since the age of three when he had watched his dad play.

Lille were 2–0 down, so Eden had nothing to lose and a great chance to impress the manager and the supporters. He attacked and attacked, running at defenders with his pace and skill. He was fearless and non-stop trouble. The crowd loved it.

'I think we did well,' Kevin Mirallas told him after the final whistle, giving him a big hug. Kevin was Belgian too and they had come on at the same time. 'We should have been starting!'

'You're right,' Eden said with confidence. 'With me on one wing and you on the other, we would have won that game.'

He was very happy and very tired. Professional football was everything that he had hoped it would be. He couldn't wait to play again, and next time for longer hopefully. The full ninety minutes was the aim.

'Do you still have time to hang out with me?'

Omar joked the next day when Eden arrived. 'You're a star now!'

'I'll always have time for you,' he promised.

There was a really good group of youngsters in the Lille squad, including Mathieu Debuchy, Adil Rami and Yohan Cabaye. Lille had finished mid-table at the end of the previous season but there were high hopes that they could become a great team in the next few years. Eden's new teammates were all very friendly and welcomed him into the group.

'So you're the kid everyone's talking about!' Yohan said when he first arrived for training. Eden was a little nervous about where he should sit in the changing room and what he should say. 'They're saying you're the missing piece in the puzzle.'

That was great to hear and Eden quickly felt at home in the squad. He was enjoying the attention of being the next big thing. However, not everyone was happy with his progress.

'He's a great player but he's really not a great trainer,' the coaches told Jean-Michel Vandamme when he checked in on his top youngster. 'We're trying to build up his strength but he doesn't listen. And he needs to improve his attitude. If things don't go his way, he often just gives up.'

This news worried Jean-Michel. Eden still had a lot to learn and he was in danger of wasting his enormous talent. He decided to have a word with him.

'Eden, how's it going?' Jean-Michel asked when he saw him in the car park. Training had only just finished and many of the younger players were still out on the pitches, practising free-kicks and crosses.

'Everything's great, thanks,' Eden replied. He was in a hurry to get home and play the new FIFA video game. Training had been boring and he just wanted to relax.

'I was just speaking to some of the coaches and they're not too pleased about your attitude.'

'Why, what did they say?' Eden was surprised that he was in trouble.

'They say you're not working hard enough,' Jean-Michel told him. He was determined to be tough with his best young player today. He needed to learn now before things got any worse.

'It's only training, though – I save my best for the matches,' was Eden's best excuse.

'That's not good enough and you know it,' Jean-Michel said angrily. He couldn't believe what he was hearing. 'Being a good footballer is only half of the picture; the other half is being a hard worker. When you have a bad day, you have to pick yourself up and do it again.'

However, it was one of the older Lille players that really made Eden change his ways. Patrick Kluivert was nearly at the end of his career when he joined the club. He had scored lots of goals for Ajax, AC Milan, Barcelona and the Netherlands national team. He was a great striker but sadly injuries had taken away his pace. He had years of experience at the highest level, so he was quick to give helpful tips to youngsters like Eden.

'You're a quality young player but you can't relax now that you're playing for the senior team,' Patrick told him one day. He didn't think that Eden was giving one hundred per cent in training and he didn't like that. 'You have to work to show you deserve your place. You have to work every single day if you want to be one of the best.'

Eden would never forget those words. Patrick was right – he needed to stay focused on his career aims and not get carried away. So far, he hadn't achieved anything. He hadn't even scored a senior goal. He still had a lot of work to do if he wanted to be as good as Kaká, Messi and Cristiano Ronaldo. So, in the next training session, he ran harder than ever before.

'How does it feel to be a Ligue 1 player now?' Kylian asked him when the family came to watch a game. At school, he had been telling all of his friends about his famous footballer brother. It was so cool.

'I'm not there yet,' Eden said with a shrug of his shoulders. 'For now, it's just great to be playing and training with the senior guys.' He was learning to be a bit more modest.

For the rest of the season, Eden moved between the youth team, the reserves and the first team. Claude Puel certainly thought he had a bright future ahead of him but he didn't want to rush things. There was plenty of time for him to develop as a player. It was great to be playing so much football but Eden was looking forward to feeling settled in one squad. It was frustrating to have different teammates all the time. As he turned seventeen, he set himself a new goal.

'This year, I want to become a regular starter for Lille,' he told his dad over dinner.

Eden had that serious look on his face again. Thierry knew he was on the verge of something great.

CHAPTER 12

PIZZA AT PINO'S

'Good afternoon, Eden! The usual for you?' the
owner of Ristorante al Ritrovo asked as he came
through the door.

'Good afternoon, Pino! Yes, please,' Eden replied,
taking his favourite seat by the window. After a hard
morning of training, it was always nice to come
and relax away from the media with one of the best
pizzas in town.

'How is Lille's number-one superstar today?'

'I feel on top of the world,' Eden said, 'but I'm
really, really hungry!'

The new season of 2008–09 was shaping up to
be a special one. Eden's hard work over the summer

had impressed everyone, including new Lille manager Rudi García.

'There are some great young players here but I think you're the best of them,' García told Eden when he called him into his office. 'The aim this year is to finish in the top five and you're going to play a key role in that. You're a proper senior player now.'

It felt so good to hear that the manager had such faith in him. Eden got the '26' shirt, which was definitely an improvement on the '33' he had worn the year before. He couldn't wait to tell Jean-Michel.

'I'm so pleased for you!' the academy director said. 'You listened to our advice and you worked hard. You deserve this.'

Eden was determined to prove his value to the team. Against Auxerre in September, when Lille were losing 2–1, he was a substitute. He was itching to play but he focused on showing his support for his teammates. It was a must-win game.

'Hazard, start warming up!' one of the coaches shouted and he jumped out of his seat. This was his chance to shine.

As Eden ran on, he was sure that he could do something special. With a few minutes to go, the ball fell to him just outside the penalty area. He was a young player and he knew that he should try to find a striker. There were lots of people in the box but it was too crowded for a pass. Eden decided to shoot instead. He took one touch to control the ball and then hit it low and hard into the bottom corner. As he turned away to celebrate, his teammates jumped on him.

'What a goal!' Yohan shouted to him. 'That's the kind of thing we need you to do in every game.'

Eden had never felt so good. The blood was pumping through his body and his heart was beating so fast. With an injury-time winner, Lille had won 3–2.

Rudi García gave him a big hug at the final whistle. 'You won that game for us, Eden. Well done.'

'Thanks for believing in me, boss!' Eden said and then he ran to join his teammates as they thanked the fans.

'Here he comes – Lille's youngest ever goal-scorer!' Mathieu cheered.

'That's the first of many!' Eden joked.

Two months later, he finally got his first league start against Saint-Étienne. He had been waiting a long time for the opportunity to play a full game.

'I hope you don't get too tired,' Thorgan said on the phone. He was really pleased for his brother but he loved to tease him. 'You must be so used to only playing twenty minutes at the end!'

'There's no chance of that,' Eden responded with a laugh. 'I've got the energy to play three games in a row!'

After twenty-five minutes of the Saint-Étienne game, he got the ball on the left and dribbled forward. As the right-back came over to tackle him, Eden did a triple stepover. His legs moved so quickly and yet the ball seemed glued to his foot. It was amazing to watch. The defender looked dizzy and as he stepped back, Eden had the space he needed to shoot. He curled the ball around the goalkeeper and into the net.

Not even Michel Bastos, Lille's Brazilian superstar, could believe the skills he'd just seen.

'Wow!' he shouted. 'Are you sure you're still only seventeen?'

Eden could barely hear his teammate over the noise of the crowd. They were cheering his name louder than ever. It was such a great feeling to be a fan favourite already.

'They'll be showing that goal on *Téléfoot* tonight!' he thought to himself.

Back in the restaurant, Eden's pizza had arrived – pepperoni and jalapeños with extra cheese. It was huge and delicious, and he never got bored of it.

'One day, you'll have to come and make it with us in the kitchen,' shouted back Eric, one of the chefs. The lunchtime rush was over and so they had the place to themselves.

'Great, sounds like fun,' Eden said. He liked cooking but he needed all of the help that he could get. 'And then in exchange, we can play football together!'

'Are you serious?' Eric replied excitedly. This was the best offer he'd ever heard. 'Can you write that down please? I want a record of what you just said.'

Eden loved to escape to Ristorante al Ritrovo. Life could be really crazy as a young, famous footballer and it was nice to have a place where he could go and feel like a normal person.

'When will we get an autographed shirt?' Pino asked, pointing up at the wall. 'Look, we've even made a space for it.'

He laughed. 'The next time I score a goal, I'll bring the shirt round for you, I promise.'

'Okay, I'll see you next weekend then!' Pino said and his staff cheered. They were all big Lille fans, especially now that one of their best customers was the star player.

CHAPTER 13

YOUNG PLAYER OF THE YEAR

'This is it,' Rudi García told his Lille players as they sat in the dressing room before the final league game of the 2008–09 season. A year earlier, Eden would have hoped to be picked for a big match like this; now, he was one of the first names on the team-sheet. 'One game to go and we have to win to finish fifth and qualify for the Europa League. We can do this!'

The pressure was on but Eden felt as confident as ever. He was determined to finish his breakthrough season in style. On a lovely May afternoon, the *Stade Pierre-Mauroy* was packed with Lille fans waving red-and-white flags. As Eden shook hands with the Nancy players, he focused on the game ahead.

'Let's get an early goal!' captain Rio Mavuba
shouted as the game started.

Eden's pass helped to set up the first goal, and
with fourteen minutes gone, Lille were 2–0 up. The
fans were dancing and singing in the sunshine – their
team would be playing in Europe next season. With
Eden causing the defenders lots of problems with his
trickery, it looked like it could be a thrashing.

But Nancy scored once and then did so again.
Suddenly, it was 2–2 and a draw wouldn't be
enough. Eden worked hard to get on the ball and
create as many chances as possible. With fifteen
minutes to go, Lille scored a third goal and this time,
they held on for the win. At the final whistle, they
celebrated like they'd won the league.

'We did it!' Yohan cheered, lifting Eden high into
the air. There was a great team spirit at the club and
it was party time.

'What a relief – I knew we could do it,' Eden said
with a big smile on his face.

What a year it had been. Eden had played thirty-
five games for Lille, which was a lot for someone so

young. He had scored six brilliant goals and set up many more for others. Whenever he got the ball, the Lille fans got excited and the opposition defenders got scared.

'I think my favourite was the goal you scored against Lyon in the Cup,' said Kylian, his brother's biggest fan. 'There were so many defenders chasing you but there was no way that you were going to lose that ball. You just kept running and then your shot was incredible.'

Eden thought for a minute. 'I think my favourite was my penalty against Toulouse. I needed to score to keep us in the shoot-out and I went for a *Panenka*! I chipped it straight down the middle but the goalkeeper couldn't reach it with his legs.'

Eden had also achieved another big personal aim; he had become a full Belgian international. French Football Federation officials had tried to persuade him to play for France instead but he didn't even consider it.

'I'm sorry but I'm a Belgian citizen,' he told them. 'I know I've played here for many years now but in my head that only makes me one per cent French and ninety-nine per cent Belgian.'

Just to make sure, Belgium's coach René Vandereycken gave Eden his debut in a friendly against Luxembourg. 'We've been watching your talent and you deserve this,' the coach told him on the phone.

Eden was so pleased to get the call-up. 'This is a dream come true,' he said to his former Lille teammate Kevin Mirallas. It was nice to see a friendly face when he arrived at the training camp. 'When I was younger, I imagined the Hazard brothers winning the World Cup for Belgium – let's make that happen!'

Eden wasn't nervous at all – he saw it as just another game. He came off the bench for the last half-hour and he almost scored with his first touch. As soon as he got the ball, he went on a weaving run through the Luxembourg defence and hit his shot just wide. He was desperate to impress so that he could play more international football.

'Congratulations, you're our seventh youngest

ever international,' captain Daniel Van Buyten told him when the game finished.

'That's not bad, but I would have loved to have been number one!' Eden joked.

Everything was going according to plan and now Eden was named as one of four players on the Ligue 1 Young Player of the Year award shortlist.

'Wow, it's such an honour to be selected – Thierry Henry and Zinedine Zidane both won it in the past,' he said when he found out. He was always looking to follow in the footsteps of his heroes.

'Good luck, even the best players find it hard to get that award!' Yohan laughed; he had been on the shortlist the previous year but had lost out to Hatem Ben Arfa.

The awards ceremony was a really fun event and all of the big names in French football were there. There were cameras everywhere and Eden really felt like a superstar. Dressed up in a tuxedo, he was glad to have Natacha there by his side.

'It would be amazing to win but it's been great

no matter what,' Eden said as they sat at their table eating a beautiful salmon dish.

'You say that now but I know you.' Natacha smiled. 'You hate losing!'

She was right, of course. Eden was desperate to be the best.

'And the winner of the Young Player of the Year award is...' the presenter said, slowly opening the envelope. The other three players on the shortlist were sitting nearby – they all looked nervous as they waited for the news.

'...Eden Hazard of Lille OSC!'

Yes! Eden kissed Natacha and made his way up to the stage to collect his award. His club teammate Michel Bastos was on the shortlist for Player of the Year and he patted Eden on the back as he passed by.

'Congratulations, mate!'

Everyone in the room was up on their feet clapping for him. Eden couldn't believe it. He made a short speech but he really didn't like talking in front of people. He was still in shock. Eden was the first international player to ever win the award. He was only eighteen but he was now the highest-rated youngster in France. Defenders would target him more than ever but he was ready to prove he wasn't a one-season wonder.

'I want more goals, more assists and more trophies,' Eden told his brothers on a family holiday. It was nice to relax and spend some time with them, but a week was long enough. He had more targets to achieve. 'And I want us to qualify for the Champions League!'

CHAPTER 14

PRAISE FROM ZIDANE

'Have you heard the news?' Thorgan said on the phone. He sounded very excited.

Eden was playing table tennis with his Lille teammates when his brother called. He was winning, of course – it was his second best sport after football. He loved basketball too but he wasn't tall enough to play. He mostly just watched his favourite NBA team, the New York Knicks, on TV instead.

'No, what's happened?' Eden asked.

'Zidane's been talking about you!'

'What?' Surely it was a joke but if it was, his brother was being really cruel.

'It's true, I'll send you the internet link,' Thorgan

added. '*Zizou* said "Hazard will be a major star in the future". For a minute I thought he was talking about me!'

Eden couldn't believe it – his number-one hero not only knew who he was but thought he would be a great player. What a special thing to hear. He read the website article again and again: 'Eden is technically gifted and very fast. He will be a major star in the future.' Eden's hands were shaking. Once he had calmed down a bit, he showed his teammates.

'Wow, that's amazing!' Yohan said. 'If I was you, I'd print that out, frame it and put it up on my wall.'

'Maybe I will,' Eden replied, although he wasn't sure that Natacha would like it above the mantelpiece.

'I bet he's recommended you to Real Madrid,' Mathieu Debuchy suggested. 'He's the Advisor to the President there now.'

Eden's brain was all over the place. It was his dream to one day play for 'Los Blancos'. The Lille chairman was telling everyone that he wasn't for sale but surely they'd let him go if Real Madrid tried to sign him. All of the big clubs in Europe were watching him and it felt great to be the focus of attention.

'I think you need at least one more season here in France,' Thierry advised. He knew how impatient and ambitious his son was but there was no need to rush things. 'Next year, you'll be ready for the pressure of a big move.'

'You're right,' Eden replied after thinking it over. 'And besides, I want to win something here at Lille before I leave.'

Eden was really enjoying the chance to play in the Europa League. It was good to challenge himself against top teams from Serbia, Belgium, Italy, Spain, Turkey and the Czech Republic.

'You seem to love scoring against any team that doesn't play in France,' Gervinho joked with him. Together, they were forming a good attacking partnership. Rather than out on the wing, Eden was now playing in the Number 10 role behind the striker. He loved the freedom to find space wherever he could. He was very comfortable with both feet and so defenders couldn't guess whether he'd go left or right.

Next up for Eden and Lille was Liverpool in March 2010. It would be a tough game and a great chance to impress the big English clubs.

'Steven Gerrard, Pepe Reina, Fernando Torres – they've got some great players,' Rio Mavuba said as they prepared for the first leg at home. 'But we've got Eden Hazard!'

Eden smiled. One day, people would talk about him as one of the best players in the world. He would make sure of that.

He was a threat throughout the game. Every time they won the ball, his teammates looked for him. When he got it, he ran forward as fast as he could, using all of his tricks. Soon Liverpool had two or three defenders marking him and they were very happy to foul him if they couldn't tackle him fairly.

'Keep going,' Rudi García told Eden as he stopped for a quick drink by the touchline. He didn't want his star player to get frustrated. 'They don't know how to handle you. The goal will come.'

He was right. With five minutes to go, Lille won a free-kick wide on the left. There was no question about who would take it. Eden took a very short run-up and curled a perfect ball into the penalty area. It went just over the heads of their attackers but it bounced awkwardly in front of Pepe Reina and skipped into the corner of the goal. Eden watched it hit the back of the net and raised his arms up in the air. What a moment. His teammates ran towards him and lifted him up high.

'You're a superstar now!' Brazilian defender Emerson shouted to him. Every Lille fan was up on their feet, making lots and lots of noise. It was like they'd won the tournament.

'Thank goodness you just signed a new contract!' Yohan joked as they celebrated the victory. 'You must be worth £30 million at least now.'

That seemed a lot of money to pay for an eighteen-year-old but the high price-tag wasn't putting anyone off.

'Barcelona, Real Madrid, Arsenal, Chelsea, Inter Milan.' Eden's agent John Bico listed just some of the clubs trying to sign him. 'They've all been following you for years now and they're all ready to pay a lot of money for you.'

'That's amazing! I'd prefer to join Real Madrid or Arsenal if possible,' Eden said.

'I know,' John replied. He knew all about Eden's love of Zidane and Henry. 'Let's wait and see. If you're named Ligue 1 Player of the Year, everything might change.'

Eden was at the big French football awards ceremony again and this time he was on the shortlist for both awards – Young Player of the Year *and* Player of the Year. A total of ten goals and even more assists was a good improvement on the previous season. He had already been selected in the Team of the Year and winning these awards would complete a fantastic season.

'Imagine if I win the Player of the Year award at this age,' he said as they waited for the presentation to begin. 'I'm still a teenager!'

'Stop, you'll jinx it!' Natacha replied.

Eden won the Young Player of the Year award and

some people thought he would complete the double. He had his doubts, however. He wasn't sure that he had done enough.

'And the winner of the Player of the Year award is...Lyon's Lisandro López!'

Eden put on a brave face and clapped for his opponent.

'I'm sorry that you didn't win,' Natacha said, giving him a kiss on the cheek. Luckily, he didn't look too upset.

'I just became the first player ever to win the Young Player of the Year twice – I can't be too disappointed, can I?' Eden told her with a smile. 'We only finished fourth in the league. You have to do better than that to win the top award. Don't worry, I'll win it next year when we win the league!'

CHAPTER 15

LEARNING LESSONS II

'Take it easy, Eden,' Natacha said as he slammed the car door. She couldn't take another journey in angry silence. 'It was just a bad day – get your head up and move on to the next game.'

'I'm having a lot of bad days at the moment,' Eden muttered. 'I don't know what's going on.'

His big plans for the new season weren't going well. He wasn't scoring goals and he wasn't feeling his normal energetic self. Expectations were so high and for the first time ever, he was having a few doubts about his talent. Lille manager Rudi García had even moved him to the bench.

'It's only for a couple of weeks,' Garcia told him in

his office. He knew how badly Eden would take the news. 'You need a bit of time to breathe and to think about your game. At the moment, you're not playing well enough but you'll be back, I'm sure of it.'

Eden couldn't believe it. He knew he was in poor form but Lille needed him. How could the team win the league without him? Unfortunately, they seemed to be doing pretty well with him not there. They were unbeaten, with Gervinho and new signing Moussa Sow scoring goals for fun. Eden was meant to be the star player, not a substitute.

'Stay calm,' Yohan said when Eden came round to play FIFA. He had never seen his teammate look so upset. 'You'll be back in the team in no time and you'll forget this bad spell ever happened.'

Eden was also struggling to make the first team for the Belgian national side. They were in a very difficult Euro 2012 qualification group with Germany and Turkey, and Eden was exactly the kind of skilful attacker they needed. However, the coach Georges Leekens didn't like his attitude, and for their game against Kazakhstan, Eden wasn't even on the bench.

'You need to work harder,' Leekens told his young star when he asked for an explanation. 'No-one can question your skills but right now, you're not showing the character that we're looking for. We need fighters out on the pitch but you don't seem to care enough. It's not just us; Lille aren't happy with you either.'

The criticism hurt but Eden could see that he needed to do better if he wanted to play regularly for both club and country. With people like Zidane talking about him, it was all too easy to relax and lose the focus that had got him there in the first place.

'Perhaps he was right that I am sometimes quite lazy in training,' he admitted to his dad once he had thought about it. 'But you know how much I hate training.'

Thierry knew that this was a moment where he had to be tough with his son. 'That's no excuse. You have faith in your ability and so do I but you have to make sure that your coaches have faith too. You have to prove yourself on the training pitch every day.'

Eden nodded. It was good to get another wake-up call – he wasn't a complete player yet and that's what he wanted to be. A big life event added to his new maturity. Eden was now a father and the responsibility of looking after his new son Yannis gave him a fresh focus on the football pitch. He worked harder than ever and soon found his club form again. He was scoring goals, he was starting every game and Lille were top of the league.

'Surely Belgium will pick you now!' Mathieu said, after Eden had set up both goals in an important win over rivals Monaco.

'I hope so,' was all Eden could say. He was doing his best to change the coach's mind about him. However, he still wasn't a starter at international level, and he couldn't understand why. He didn't come on at all against Austria and then he only played half an hour against Azerbaijan. He understood that he was still young but he was desperate to play a bigger role in the qualification campaign.

'Why am I still on the bench?' he asked Belgium's assistant manager Marc Wilmots.

'Talent isn't enough at the top level,' Wilmots

replied. He hoped that harsh words would inspire Eden to even greater things. 'You can change a match at any moment but you have to work on your consistency. In France, all they talk about are your moments of magic. They don't talk about the times you disappear and don't help the team.'

Eden knew that it was good advice but he still felt that it was a bit unfair.

'They just don't like me,' he told Rudi García when he returned to France. 'I'll work even harder but I don't think it'll be enough.'

'There is plenty of room for improvement but they shouldn't forget that you're only nineteen years old. I know you're angry but show it in the best way possible – on the pitch for Lille,' Rudi replied.

CHAPTER 16

TREBLE TIME

'I'll take this,' Eden said, putting the ball down. Lille had won a free-kick in the last minute of the first-half. They were drawing 0–0 away at Nancy but it was the kind of match that *Les Dogues* needed to win if they wanted to be Ligue 1 champions for the first time in fifty-seven years. Eden and Gervinho had been linking up well all game but the goalkeeper had made some good saves to stop them.

Eden took a deep breath and focused on the target. He was standing on the left side of the penalty area, in a similar position to the free-kick he had scored against Liverpool in the Europa League. He would need to curl it with his right foot over the wall and into the bottom corner of the net. Eden had been doing this for years, ever since he was a small boy playing for Royal Stade Brainois.

He took a short run-up and hit the ball powerfully. The Nancy players in the wall jumped high but they couldn't reach it. It flew over their heads, swerved through the air and sailed past the goalkeeper's stretching arms. The crowd went wild and Eden's teammates ran to celebrate with him. Gervinho was first to arrive.

'You don't even get that excited about scoring anymore!' he said, giving Eden a high-five and a hug.

'I know, it's just normal now,' he replied with a smile. It was his seventh league goal of the season and his twelfth in all competitions. Every year he was adding more goals to his game.

He loved scoring big, match-winning goals. A few weeks earlier he had scored the first goal in Lille's French Cup semi-final win over Nice. After a great one-two, he hit a brilliant strike into the top of the net. Lille were on track for an amazing league and cup double and Eden was playing the key role he had always dreamt about. After a difficult first half of the season, he was now playing better than ever.

'We've got four league matches left and a Cup Final. Five more wins – we can do this!' he told his teammates in the changing room after the Nancy victory. There was a great team spirit at the club and a growing confidence too. They really believed that they could do it.

Eden set up the winner against Saint-Étienne and then Gervinho scored the only goal against Sochaux. The team was getting a little nervous but they were still winning games.

'We're so nearly there,' Eden said to Yohan as they prepared for the Cup Final. 'Only Paris Saint-Germain are standing in our way now.'

'Yes but they're a very good team,' Yohan replied. They had top French internationals like Claude Makélélé and Ludovic Giuly and Lille could certainly not expect an easy game in the league or in the Cup.

The Cup Final was a very tense match. No-one wanted to make a single mistake that could lose the game for their team and so there were very few chances for either side. As he stood on the massive Stade de France pitch with his teammates before kick-off, Eden felt a few nerves for the first time in months. This was his first final and he was desperate to be the matchwinner. However, he found it very difficult to find the space he needed to create something special. Instead, it was his teammate Ludovic Obraniak who became the hero.

With two minutes to go, it was still 0–0 and the Lille supporters were cheering loudly for a goal. They won a free-kick near the corner flag on the right. Normally Eden would have taken the free-kick but from that position, it was much better for a left-footed player to curl the ball into the box.

Eden stood towards the edge of the area and waited for any rebounds. Instead, Ludovic's free-kick drifted straight over the goalkeeper's head and into the net. It was a strange goal but they didn't mind at all. As soon as it landed, the Lille players ran towards Ludovic as fast as their tired legs could take them. He slid along the grass and Eden was one of the first to jump on top of him. He had never heard the fans make quite so much noise.

'Did you mean to do that?' Eden shouted to Ludovic.

He shrugged. 'Who cares? We've scored!'

The celebrations after the final whistle went on for hours. It was fifty-six years since Lille had won the French Cup. It was a fantastic day for the club and Eden was so pleased to be a big part of it.

'It wasn't my best game but we won and that's all that matters!' he told his brothers when they met up with him later. Eden still had a huge smile on his face. 'Now I've got a league title to go and win!'

One point in the league match against Paris Saint-Germain would be enough for Lille to lift the trophy. However, PSG would certainly be out for revenge after the Cup Final defeat. Eden couldn't create a winning goal but a 2–2 scoreline was enough. As the match came to an end, there was a mighty roar from the crowd. The Lille players celebrated with each other and then ran to share their joy with the fans.

Eden could even see Belgian flags amongst the red-and-white Lille scarves.

'What a moment!' he said to Yohan as they jumped up and down in front of the supporters. The team formed a conga line and danced around the edge of the pitch.

'You'll have many more of these,' his teammate predicted. Everyone at Lille knew that Eden was destined for even greater things one day.

Eventually, Eden found Natacha and they kissed.

'I told you!' he shouted to her, laughing. 'I told you we'd win the league this year!'

'You did indeed,' Natacha nodded. She was so happy for her partner. 'So what's next?'

'Tomorrow, I'm going to complete the treble!'

Eden had been nominated for the Ligue 1 Player of the Year award again and this time he believed that he had a great chance of winning. He was up against his Lille teammate Moussa Sow, who had scored twenty-five goals but Eden had faith that this was his year.

'And the winner is…' the announcer began,

opening the envelope up on the stage, '...Lille's Eden Hazard!'

What a season it had turned out to be. As he collected the award, Eden said a silent thanks to the Belgian national team coaches who had inspired him to keep on improving. With their criticisms in his head, he had succeeded in playing his way into the record books – the youngest ever Ligue 1 Player of the Year.

CHAPTER 17

LAST SEASON AT LILLE

Joe Cole couldn't believe what he was watching. He had just arrived at Lille on a season loan from Liverpool and this was his first training session. He knew how skilful players in France could be but the kid he was watching was a different class.

'Wow, Eden's got everything!' he told his Liverpool teammates when he returned to England for a few days. Joe thought that the club should do everything possible to sign him before Barcelona or Real Madrid made a proper offer. 'He's a bit like Messi – he's stocky and he's got strong legs, an amazing touch and a great finish too.'

'Yes, we know all about him,' Steven Gerrard

replied. 'He scored the winner against us in the Europa League a couple of years ago.'

'I remember he was a very cocky lad,' Jamie Carragher added.

'You're right but all of the top players have that confidence,' Joe argued. 'He's fearless and he knows exactly how good he is.'

Despite all of the transfer rumours, Eden had decided to stay at Lille for one more season. They had given him the Number 10 shirt to show him just how important he was to the team. Yohan, Gervinho and Adil Rami had all signed for bigger clubs in England and Spain over the summer, but Eden had a few last goals to achieve at the club.

'I want to play in the Champions League here,' he told Mathieu, 'and I want to see if we can defend the league title.'

Eden was still only twenty-one and there was still one area of his game in particular that he wanted to improve before he took on his next challenge.

'If I want to play as a Number 10 for one of the best teams in the world, I need to score more goals,' he said at the last family dinner in Belgium before his return to France.

'Okay, so what's your target this season?' Thierry asked. He knew how important development was for his son. If he had an aim in his head, there was no stopping him.

'Twenty,' he replied straight away.

'That's a lot when you're not a proper striker,' Thorgan suggested. 'You create a lot of goals too.'

'I know, but I'm sure I can get twenty goals in all competitions,' Eden replied. 'Without Gervinho, they'll need me to score more.'

It was a lot of pressure to put on himself but he wanted to take more responsibility at Lille. By Christmas, he had already equalled his previous Ligue 1 season best of seven goals but he wasn't satisfied.

'I didn't score any in the Champions League and we're out already,' Eden told his brothers. 'And at this rate we might not qualify for next season. I didn't score in the league for over two months – I can't be that inconsistent.'

Thorgan and Kylian were impressed by their brother's focus. He had always aimed high but they had never heard Eden being so tough on himself.

'You're only at the halfway point,' Kylian said, trying to cheer him up. 'You've got more than twenty games still to play.'

One skill that Eden didn't need to work on was penalties. He was now Lille's first-choice taker and he loved it. Against Ajaccio in December 2011, they had won a late penalty with the score at 2–2. The pressure was on to be the matchwinner but Eden calmly faked to shoot in the corner and then chipped it cheekily over the diving goalkeeper.

'Another *Panenka*!' Mathieu cheered as they celebrated. Eden had taken a penalty like that before in the French Cup against Toulouse. 'You're the coolest guy I know.'

'Penalties are fun!' Eden told him. 'It's a one-on-one battle and you just have to hold your nerve. If you do, you'll score every time.'

With one match left in the season, he had scored a total of nineteen goals.

'I really didn't think you'd make it,' Thorgan said, although he knew that he should never bet against his brother.

'I haven't yet,' Eden replied. He was determined to make this a final game to remember.

Eden didn't yet know which team he would sign for but he would not be playing for Lille next season. It was time for him to move on. On 20 May 2011, he played his final game for the club, against Nancy. The *Stade Pierre-Mauroy* was packed with fans wanting to say goodbye to their star player after seven great years at the club. They cheered his name from the first minute to the last.

Eden was captain for the day and he made it a very special day for everyone. His first goal was a great striker's finish. He ran on to a great through-ball and calmly placed the ball past the goalkeeper. He had reached his target of twenty goals and to celebrate, he blew kisses to the crowd.

'More! More! More!' they shouted back to him.

His second goal was almost identical. Now, he had two and he wanted that first ever professional hat-trick. A few minutes later, Lille won a penalty and everyone knew who would take it. Eden stood with hands on hips, waiting for the referee to blow his whistle. He wasn't nervous at all because he knew that he would score. He cleverly sent the goalkeeper the wrong way and the ball went into the bottom corner.

Eden held his arms above his head and his teammates lifted him high into the air. Every fan in the stadium was on their feet, clapping. It was such a perfect way to end his time at Lille.

With a minute left, Eden was substituted. As he left the field, his teammates all ran over to hug him. It was even more emotional than he had expected it to be – he'd had a great time at the club. Eden clapped to the thousands of Lille supporters. He was so grateful for all of their love. Once the match was over, he made a speech on the pitch.

'Thank you so much, I will miss you all!' Eden said as he looked at his teammates and coaches stood near him but also the fans behind them. It was a very happy day but also a sad one.

Eden had achieved everything he could in French football. He had won the league, the Cup, two Young Player of the Year awards and he completed the season with a second Player of the Year award in a row. It was now time for the next step, but which of the biggest clubs in Europe would win the race for Eden?

CHAPTER 18

CHASED
BY CHELSEA

Guy Hillion had lost count of the number of times that he had watched Eden play for Lille. It was somewhere between twenty and thirty, he thought. As Chelsea's chief scout in France, it was his job to find the best new talents and Guy had been recommending the Belgian playmaker for years.

'There's really no weakness,' he told the club after yet another perfect report. If they didn't act soon, another club would buy him. 'Eden can play on either wing or in the Number 10 role. He can create goals and he can score them too. He's got a great touch, great vision and great skill. He's not always the best team player but you just need to

manage the kid in the right way. He'll be a star,
I promise.'

By 2012, Eden had become Chelsea's number-one
transfer target. When Roberto Di Matteo took over as
manager in March, the club were fifth in the Premier
League and twenty points behind leaders Manchester
City. Worst of all, they were in danger of missing out
on a Champions League spot for the next season.

'The football we're playing is boring,' Di Matteo
told his assistant, Eddie Newton. 'The fans want
entertainment. Where are all our creative attacking
players?'

'We do have Juan Mata,' Eddie replied.

'Yes, but that's not enough,' the Italian manager
said. 'We need three or four players like that.'

Eden knew all about Chelsea's interest but he
wanted to play Champions League football and
he wanted to sign for a team that played exciting
football.

'Arsenal and Real Madrid are still my favourites,'
he told his agent John Bico. 'Have they made offers
yet?'

John shook his head. 'No, maybe they think £30 million is too much to pay for you. If so, they're wrong. Chelsea and Manchester United are leading the race at the moment. Which would you prefer?'

It was a difficult decision and Eden needed time. 'I just don't know,' he replied.

Thanks to Guy's advice, Chelsea tried everything to sign him. Di Matteo himself came to speak to Eden, saying: 'We're building a new team, one that will play beautiful football. We want to be the biggest team in Europe and we want you to be the star.'

Eden was impressed by the club's manager but he was even more impressed by the club's owner. He had intended to go and watch a film at the famous Cannes festival but in the end he had to cancel.

'Why, what are you doing instead?' his Lille teammates asked him. They were disappointed that he wasn't joining them.

'I've got a meeting on Roman Abramovich's yacht,' Eden told them eventually after lots of questions. He was trying to keep quiet about the transfer dealings but he didn't want to lie to his friends.

Abramovich greeted him like an old friend and treated him like a superstar. Champagne, sun and sea – Eden could get used to this lifestyle. 'You're the playmaker we need to reach the highest level,' Abramovich told him. 'Our fans will love you. Don't think about other offers – this is the best offer you will ever get!'

It felt good to be the top target for such a big club. Eden was starting to picture himself playing in the blue shirt at Stamford Bridge. The third part of Chelsea's masterplan was even more successful. Eden was enjoying some family time back in Belgium when he got a call from Gervinho.

'Hi mate, how's it going?' he answered.

'I'm well, thanks. I've got someone here who wants to talk to you,' Gervinho said.

After a short pause, Eden heard another voice on the phone. 'Hi, this is Didier Drogba.'

Didier Drogba? Eden couldn't believe it – why did one of the best strikers in the world want to speak to him?

'I hear Chelsea have made an offer and you're

thinking about it,' Didier continued. 'Signing for Chelsea was the best decision that I ever made. I've had eight amazing years here. Come join us! It's a great club and the fans are incredible. Believe me; you can reach the same level as Messi and Ronaldo here.'

That was exactly what Eden wanted – a team where he could develop from the next big thing into a truly world-class player. He decided to talk to his father.

'It's got to be your decision,' Thierry said, 'but it's clear that Chelsea are desperate to sign you and that's very important.'

'You're right,' Eden replied, 'and I think I have a better chance of playing every game there than I would at Manchester United. They've got a young team but it's a project and they're really ambitious. My one worry is that they might not be in the Champions League next season.'

'Why don't you wait and see what happens at the end of the season?' his father suggested. That seemed like a good idea and gave Eden more time to think.

Chelsea had finished the 2011–12 Premier League

season in sixth place but they had won the FA Cup
and they reached the Champions League final against
Bayern Munich. If they won that, Chelsea would be
able to play in next year's competition. Eden had his
fingers firmly crossed as he watched the final on TV
with his family.

It was a dull match and when Thomas Müller
scored in the eighty-third minute, it looked like
Chelsea were about to lose.

'Shall I call Sir Alex Ferguson?' Thorgan asked,
but Eden wasn't in the mood for jokes.

But with two minutes to go, Chelsea equalised
and the scorer was Didier, the man who had called
him to persuade him to join the club. It was the most
powerful header that Eden had ever seen. He jumped
off the sofa to celebrate the goal. Playing alongside
Didier would be amazing.

'You're a Chelsea fan already!' Kylian said,
laughing at his brother's excitement.

It went to penalties and Didier was the last of
Chelsea's five takers. If he scored, they would win
the Champions League. Eden was so nervous that he

could hardly watch. Didier stepped up and calmly sent the goalkeeper the wrong way. It was a penalty that Eden would have been very proud of. As the Chelsea players ran to celebrate, he turned to his family.

'Right, I've made up my mind!'

A week later, Eden chose to tell the world through Twitter. His tweet was read by millions of people in a few hours.

'I'm signing for the Champions League winner,' was all it said.

CHAPTER 19

WELCOME TO THE PREMIER LEAGUE

Eden couldn't wait to get started at Chelsea. Belgium hadn't qualified for Euro 2012 and so he had a full pre-season to prepare himself for his first Premier League season. As Andrés Iniesta and his Spanish teammates lit up the tournament in Poland and Ukraine, Eden was settling into life in London.

'The weather isn't great but I'm sure we'll be happy here,' he said to Natacha as they decorated their beautiful new home.

'Yes, we just need to find a good French restaurant!' she joked.

'Good idea – I'll ask Florent Malouda when he gets back from the Euros.'

A few weeks later, Eden was off to the USA for preseason friendlies. His new teammates were a very friendly group, with players from all over the world, and there was a fun atmosphere on the tour.

'Welcome to the Champions League winners!' Brazilians David Luiz and Ramires told him with big smiles on their faces. They loved playing tricks on each other. 'With you in our team, we can win it again!'

Eden had every reason to feel at home. He was Chelsea's fourth young Belgian, along with goalkeeper Thibaut Courtois, midfielder Kevin De Bruyne and striker Romelu Lukaku.

'We're the future of this club!' they cheered as they sat at dinner together. By the end of July, they had a fifth member and one that Eden knew very well.

'The transfer is complete,' Thorgan shouted excitedly on the phone. 'Chelsea now have two Hazards!'

Eden was very pleased for his brother and happy to have family around him as he took on his biggest challenge yet. The pressure was on; £32 million was one of the Premier League's biggest ever transfer fees.

'You're going to be great here, don't worry,' Fulham's Belgian midfielder Mousa Dembélé said when they met up for a coffee. 'You always need a little time to adapt to a new style of football but it won't take you long. You're not the biggest footballer but it hasn't stopped David Silva, Juan Mata and Luka Modrić, has it?'

That was good to hear. By the start of the 2012–13 season, Eden was the only Belgian left at Chelsea. Thibaut Courtois, Kevin Mirallas, Romelu Lukaku and and Eden's brother Thorgan had all gone out on loan.

'I'm glad that I'm still here,' Eden told Natacha. 'It shows that the manager has faith in me. I don't need to go anywhere else to learn – I'm ready for this!'

Chelsea's new season started with an away trip to Wigan and Eden was in the starting line-up.

'Welcome to the Premier League!' Juan Mata joked as they warmed up. 'I warn you, it'll be a really tough debut.'

The defenders gave him a few early kicks but Eden wasn't going to let that stop him. Within the first ten minutes, he had set up the first goal and then won a penalty for the second.

'Wow, that was outstanding,' Di Matteo told him at half-time with a smile. He had a very good feeling about his new signing.

When Eden was substituted with half an hour to go, the Chelsea fans stood up and cheered for their new hero. It was great to hear but Eden was too tired to thank them properly.

'I thought the football would be a lot more physical here than in France but that's not the big difference. It's the intensity,' he told his dad afterwards. 'There's no breathing space – it's one hundred per cent all the time. Teams don't pass the ball around in defence and give the attackers a chance to rest.'

'Well, you better get used to that!' Thierry

replied. Laziness was not allowed in the Hazard family.

A week later, Chelsea played against Newcastle at home. Fernando Torres won a penalty and with Frank Lampard on the bench, Eden had the chance to score his first goal for the club. With 40,000 fans behind him, he calmly struck the ball into the bottom corner. Eden pumped his fist – it felt good to be off the mark.

He was a famous superstar but Eden liked a quiet life off the pitch. He had been with Natacha since they were fourteen years old and she was now pregnant with their second child. Eden decided it was time to show her just how important she was to him.

'You're my best friend and the mother of my children,' he told her over dinner one night. 'I couldn't do all of this without you. I love you so much – will you marry me?'

With tears of joy in her eyes, Natacha said yes but she didn't want a big, flashy wedding. Eden agreed and so they had a small ceremony with family and friends. It was a perfect day and the newspapers only found out when they noticed the ring on Eden's finger.

'Oh well, at least no journalists turned up at the wedding!' the new Mrs Hazard laughed.

When Chelsea were playing well, Eden was at the centre of everything, setting up goals with his amazing dribbling skills. He was a joy to watch as he ran past defenders again and again. However, when Chelsea were struggling, sometimes he didn't support his teammates as much as he should.

'I hate defending,' Eden told Juan in training. 'That's not my job!'

Juan disagreed. 'No, everyone has to defend in this league. There's nothing the fans hate more than seeing one of their players just walking around the pitch. You get paid a lot of money and so you have to work hard.'

Eden understood but he was frustrated. He just wanted to do what he did best – attack.

In the League Cup against Swansea, Chelsea

had ten minutes left to score two goals. Eden was desperate to win the game for his team and for the fans. They won a corner but the Swansea ballboy grabbed the ball and tried to waste as much time as possible. Eden was furious – it was cheating.

When the ballboy lay on top of the ball, Eden kicked the ball out from under him. But the ballboy claimed that he had kicked him in the ribs and the Swansea players were furious. When the referee called him over and gave him a red card, Eden couldn't believe it.

'I was trying to get the ball!' he kept saying, but it didn't matter. The sending-off was one of the lowest points in Eden's career. He hated to make the headlines for the wrong reasons.

'I just want to do my best for Chelsea,' he told Frank Lampard. 'I want to entertain the fans, that's all.'

'I know you do and you will,' Frank said, putting his arm around Eden. He liked to give useful advice to the younger players. 'Trust me, you've got absolutely everything and you're only twenty-two.

You've got the world at your feet and you scare the life out of defenders. Don't let this get you down; let it motivate you to work even harder to get even better.'

CHAPTER 20

THE SPECIAL ONE

Rumours had been spreading for months. Who would become the next Chelsea manager? Would 'The Special One', José Mourinho, really return to Stamford Bridge?

'I hope that's true,' Frank Lampard said as they waited to hear. 'He's the best manager I've ever worked with. Between 2004 and 2006, we were an amazing team thanks to him.'

Eden wanted to work with the top coaches in the world and Mourinho was the very best. It was a very exciting prospect. The previous season, Chelsea had won the Europa League and they came close to winning the FA and League Cups too. What they needed now was someone who could take them to the next level.

'He's so good at working with players,' Frank continued. 'He understands how to get the best out of everyone.'

That's what Eden needed. After a first season of highs and lows, he wanted to become more consistent this year, and consistently great. 'The Special One' could help him with that.

Mourinho's arrival was the big news of the summer and expectations were very high. He wanted all of the Chelsea players to understand his ideas from the start.

'I'm back because I love this club and because I believe we can achieve great things,' he told them at his first team meeting. There was total silence in the room. Even David Luiz was paying attention. 'This is a young squad with a lot of talent. We have to improve but not by spending lots of money on new players; we have to improve by working hard. I look forward to working with you and if you're willing to learn and you give me one hundred-and-ten per cent, you'll enjoy working with me too.'

At this point, Mourinho smiled. On TV and in the newspapers, he always seemed very cold and arrogant but Eden quickly found out that he wasn't like that in real life. He was funny and he cared about his players.

'I have big plans for you,' Mourinho told Eden, putting an arm around him in training. 'You can be a world-class player for us but you need to listen and play for the team, not just for yourself. We need to turn your talent into more goals, more assists and more important performances. I hope you're ready. I don't make life easy for my great players!'

Two new signings, the Brazilian Willian and the German André Schürrle, played similar positions but as long as Eden played well, the Number 10 role would be his. He was determined to please his new manager with his footballing skills but also with his attitude.

'He's taken me under his wing,' Eden told his dad

on the phone. 'José says that he'll make sure that I'm in the same league as Messi and Ronaldo!'

However, he wasn't going to get any special treatment. When Eden missed a training session before a big Champions League match, he was left out of the squad. He was very disappointed to watch from the stands as Chelsea won comfortably without him. It was especially tough to see Willian and André playing so well in his position behind the striker.

'You're still a kid and kids make mistakes,' Mourinho told him after the match. 'I'm trying to educate you in the best way possible. You wanted to play and so I didn't let you play. That's made you upset but hopefully you've thought about what you've done wrong and you'll be ready to make up for it on Saturday.'

Eden nodded; he understood his manager's message. It was time to show the appropriate spirit to match his skill.

A cold, wet Wednesday night match at Sunderland in December wasn't an easy game. It was the kind of match where critics expected a small, talented player to sulk and stay away from the physical battle. But Eden was determined that this wouldn't happen this time.

He set up Chelsea's first goal by dribbling into the box and pulling back a lovely cross for Frank to head into the net.

'What a ball!' Frank shouted, running over to thank Eden for the assist.

Fifteen minutes later, he was running down the left again, taking on the Sunderland defence. César Azpilicueta was making an overlapping run and Eden pretended to pass to him but cut inside instead. On the edge of the penalty area, he hit a fierce, dipping shot into the bottom corner.

The Chelsea fans went crazy. It was the kind of solo goal that Eden had scored so many times for Lille but it was nice to be doing it for Chelsea too now. He jumped into the air with his arms thrown towards the sky. Eden looked at the touchline and he could see Mourinho smiling. He wasn't done yet.

In the second half, Eden got the ball on the wing

but he was being double-marked now. He waited for support and slipped the ball through to Frank, who flicked it beautifully back into his path. Eden dribbled across the penalty area, with the Sunderland defenders trailing behind him. He was off-balance but he fired a great shot past the goalkeeper, and was so pleased with the goal that he took his shirt off and threw it in the air.

'That yellow card was worth it!' he joked with Juan.

At the final whistle, Mourinho gave Eden a big hug. 'Wow, that was your best performance yet – you showed ambition from the first minute until the last. You're unplayable when you're that determined.'

Eden was on cloud nine. He was scoring goals and winning games in the best league in the world, and everyone loved him. His dreams were coming true. He even scored a hat-trick against Newcastle to become Chelsea's leading scorer.

'I feel like a much better player now,' he told his brothers when they came for a London visit. They were both back playing in Belgium, Thorgan on loan from Chelsea at Zulte Waregem and Kylian at White Star Bruxelles. 'I'm stronger and I'm cleverer – I'm learning how to be the matchwinner.'

Mourinho was happy with Eden's progress in attack but there was still work to be done on his efforts in defence. In the semi-final of the Champions League against Atlético Madrid, Chelsea had a great chance to get to a second final in a row. But after taking the lead, they lost 3–1. Mourinho was furious and he blamed Eden in particular.

'Their first goal was your fault because you didn't mark the right-back,' he told him angrily. 'How many times have I told you? You have to protect your left-back and you have to concentrate at all times.'

Eden knew he had made a big mistake in such an important match but he was really trying to improve his defensive work. The fans understood; they voted him Chelsea's Player of the Year. He was Chelsea's top scorer with seventeen goals and he won the PFA Young Player of the Year award too. Eden wasn't the complete player yet but he was getting near.

CHAPTER 21

BELGIANS IN BRAZIL

'The newspapers say that we're one of the favourites to win,' Romelu Lukaku told the Belgium players as they gathered to head off to the 2014 World Cup in Brazil. It was strange to hear people talk about Belgium alongside the likes of Brazil, Argentina and Germany. They hadn't even qualified for an international tournament since World Cup 2002, but now they had one of the best young teams in the world.

Their experienced captain Vincent Kompany was used to playing under that kind of pressure, and said: 'We've got a great side – there's no reason we can't win!'

Eden really believed in his teammates; they had pace, power and strength in depth. After a difficult couple of years at international level, he had finally become a key figure in the Belgium first XI. He had scored two goals in qualification, including the winner against Macedonia. A header landed right at his feet on the edge of the penalty area. He had time to take a shot at goal but instead he calmly dribbled past two defenders and hit a great left-footed shot into the bottom corner.

'What an important goal,' Christian Benteke said as they celebrated. 'Brazil, here we come!'

The atmosphere at the tournament was incredible. Eden couldn't wait to get out on the pitch and play for his country. He had grown up watching his hero Zidane winning the 1998 World Cup for France. It was the greatest stage, with millions of people watching. Eden would never forget the sights and sounds of thirty-two sets of fans from all over the world. He was already doing the maths in his head – 'If I'm lucky, I might be able to play at four World Cups like Enzo Scifo.'

'Lucky you,' Vincent said, 'I'm already twenty-eight so it might be now or never!'

Eden felt quite tired after another long Premier League season but he was desperate to play well and enjoy the experience. A lot of the Belgium players were in their prime and it might be the best chance they would get. Christian couldn't play in the tournament because of an injury and so Eden and Romelu needed to be the team's main goalscorers.

'We might not get to play together at Chelsea very often but I think we've got a good understanding – you create the goals and I score them!' Romelu joked as they prepared for the first-round matches.

Against Algeria, Belgium were desperately looking for a winning goal. Eden ran forward on the counter-attack and he could see that they had three attackers against two defenders. Romelu was being marked closely but Dries Mertens was in space on the right. Eden played the ball across the penalty area and Dries scored with a great finish.

'We were lucky today,' manager Marc Wilmots said after the game. He wasn't happy with the way his team had started. 'We need more from every single one of you.'

Eden was the one player that Wilmots praised. 'You can be one of the five best players in the world – you have everything you need.'

'Thanks, Coach,' Eden replied. 'I don't think I deserve it at the moment but that's what I'm aiming for. Messi and Ronaldo score goals in almost every game and that's what I need to do.'

Eden was the hero again in the next game against Russia. It was 0–0 with two minutes left when he got the ball on the left. Eden knew it was his responsibility to do something special to unlock a well-organised defence. There were two Russians near him but he skipped past both of them and ran towards the goal. As he reached the touchline, he pulled the ball back and Divock Origi smashed it into the net.

A lot of the players ran to celebrate with Divock but Kevin De Bruyne hugged Eden instead. 'That was world class, mate – thanks to you, we're through to the next round!'

With a victory over South Korea, Belgium had
now won three games out of three but in each game
by just one goal. The opponents would only get
harder from now on as they entered the later rounds.
Eden, in particular, was looking to improve.

'I've had a few great moments so far but I haven't
played a great ninety minutes yet,' he discussed with
Wilmots as they prepared for the next round.

'I agree,' the coach replied. 'I don't want to put
too much pressure on you because you're still young.
But I know what you can do. I want to see you really
take hold of a game.'

'It's not always easy to find the space,' Eden
argued. 'We're looking strong in defence but in
attack, we're still learning to play together.'

Wilmots didn't want to hear any excuses. 'You
have the quality to find gaps and score goals – I have
confidence in you and so does all of Belgium.'

It was nice to know that his coach had faith in him.
Eden loved the excitement of the knock-out stages,
when every match was a must-win. He was desperate
to be the national hero but Belgium's opponents,

the USA, were a much-improved team and again he struggled to create chances. As the game went on, Eden became more and more frustrated.

'Just keep playing your natural game,' Wilmots told him on the touchline. 'You're trying too hard to do something amazing by yourself. The USA defence see you as the main threat so use that to make space for Divock, Romelu and Kevin.'

In extra-time, Kevin managed to shoot across the goal. Eden was there at the back post but he didn't need to touch it – it was already in the net.

Eden ran to celebrate with Kevin. '*That* was world class!' he shouted.

Ten minutes later, Eden played Kevin through down the left wing. He passed to Romelu, who hit a powerful shot past the goalkeeper.

'What a great team goal!' Romelu said with a big smile on his face.

In the quarter-finals, Belgium faced Argentina. Eden was going head-to-head with Messi, one of his favourite players. Like Messi, he was expected to be his country's leading attacker.

'I haven't scored yet and that's not good enough,' he told Vincent during the build-up to the big game. 'I'm getting closer, though. If you can stop Messi, I promise I'll make sure we get a goal!'

'That's a deal!' Vincent said. 'This is the biggest game of our lives – tonight, we can make history.'

Eden felt the goosebumps on his skin as he lined up in front of nearly 70,000 fans to sing the national anthem. Vincent was right – this really was the biggest game of his life. With his hand on his heart, Eden focused on what he needed to do – attack, create and score.

Within eight minutes, Argentina had the lead. Eden was playing through the middle in his preferred Number 10 position and he tried to take control of the game but Barcelona's Javier Mascherano followed him everywhere. After seventy-five disappointing minutes, Wilmots made the brave decision to substitute Eden. It was a bad way to leave the World Cup but he had given everything and he had learnt a lot.

'We'll bounce back,' he told Romelu as they got

ready to return to Chelsea. 'The early goal made it difficult and we were unlucky not to score an equaliser. Brazil could have gone better but we had a good tournament. It's a young squad and we'll be older, wiser and better next time!'

CHAPTER 22

EDEN'S BIG SEASON

'This is going to be my season,' Eden told Mourinho with his usual confidence. 'I need to score more goals and we need to be champions. With me, Cesc and Diego we can beat every team!'

Chelsea had signed Cesc Fàbregas and Diego Costa over the summer of 2014 and Eden was excited to play in the same team as such great players. Cesc would start the attacks from midfield and Diego would get the goals that they needed. They would help Eden to reach the very top level.

'We've only been training together for a few weeks but it's like we've been playing together for years,' he told his dad on the phone.

Chelsea had their strongest team in years and everyone got on really well.

'Are you really only twenty-five?' Eden asked Diego. He couldn't believe that this big, powerful man that they called 'The Beast' was only a couple of years older than him. 'You look at least thirty-five!'

'With your height you look about twelve!' Diego replied, giving him a friendly jostle.

Chelsea started well and Eden was at the centre of everything. He was now wearing the '10' shirt, the same number as his hero Zinedine Zidane, and he was living up to his reputation as the Premier League's most dangerous playmaker. With his dribbling, Cesc's passing and Diego's shooting, Chelsea were unbeaten and top of the table.

Against Crystal Palace, Chelsea were struggling to break through a ten-man defence. They were passing the ball back and forth when suddenly Cesc passed to Eden, who flicked it on to Oscar, after which Oscar passed it back to Cesc who ran into the penalty area and scored. It was an amazing team goal and the fans went wild.

'One-touch football – that's the new Chelsea!' Cesc shouted as they celebrated another victory.

Eden was scoring lots of goals as well as setting them up. Even with Diego in the team, he was still the penalty taker and he was very proud of his hundred per cent record.

'I've got sixteen out of sixteen,' he told Cesc. 'I'm the only player in Europe who has taken more than fifteen penalties and scored all of them.'

During the busy, important Christmas period, Eden was Chelsea's star man. Against Stoke, he kept going even when they fouled him badly. Mourinho was impressed by his player's improvement.

'That was fantastic!' he told Eden after the game. 'You gave everything, including your body, for that win. A year ago, you wouldn't have battled like that but now you're a fighter and a real team player.'

Eden had grown stronger but without losing any of his flair. He was every right-back's worst nightmare because they never knew what he would do next. Sometimes he ran down the left wing and sometimes he went into the centre on his right foot. Sometimes he dribbled around defenders and sometimes he played a killer pass or hit a powerful shot.

Chelsea were 1–0 down at Southampton and they needed their Number 10 to do something special. Cesc played a great pass over the top and Eden was through on goal. There were two defenders near him but he cut inside past both of them and shot into the bottom corner. It was a magical goal but that was normal these days for Eden.

'I'm getting consistent,' he told Natacha happily. 'That's always been my problem – in the past I would do something great in one game and then nothing for a few weeks. Now, I'm doing it almost every game.'

If he could keep it up, he could reach the level of Messi and Ronaldo. Eden was sure of that. Mourinho had always been tough with him but they wanted the same thing: perfection. He was learning every day from his manager in training and it was now showing on the pitch. All of the hard work and criticism had been worth it.

Eden's reward was a big new five-year contract. 'I'm very happy because I'm playing for one of the best clubs in the world,' he told the media. In March 2015, Chelsea were still top of the league and also in the final of the League Cup against Tottenham.

'I want another winner's medal!' Eden told Cesc. 'I came here to win trophies and so far I've only won the Europa League. We keep getting close but that's not good enough.'

It was an incredible day at Wembley. As he ran on to the pitch, Eden could see thousands of blue Chelsea flags waving in the stands. He really wanted to give the fans a match-winning performance and he worked hard all game. Eden didn't score but it was a great team effort. They all celebrated together on the pitch afterwards, with Mourinho at the centre. Eden had never seen him look so pleased.

'Well done lads!' he shouted. 'This is just the start, though. We have the Champions League and the Premier League to win now.'

Eden didn't need to be told – he was already thinking ahead to the next match and the next victory. Against West Ham, Cesc played the ball out to Ramires who put in a lovely cross. Eden had made a great striker's run from the back post and he headed it powerfully past the keeper. It was the winning goal but it was also special for other reasons.

'A header? I'm not sure I've ever seen you head the ball!' Mourinho joked after the final whistle.

Eden smiled – it was only the third headed goal of his whole career. 'Thanks to you, I've got lots of new skills now!'

CHAPTER 23

PLAYER OF
THE YEAR

'If we beat Manchester United today, we'll only need another couple of wins to get the title,' Eden told the Chelsea team in the dressing room. In the past, he had been a quiet squad player but now he was one of the team leaders. He was enjoying his new responsibility.

Chelsea were out of the Champions League and so full focus was on the Premier League. With Diego injured, Eden had become their main playmaker *and* goalscorer. He was determined not to let anyone down.

With Manchester United looking for a Top Four finish to the season, Chelsea had to defend really well. Even Eden was back helping his left-back César Azpilicueta. Near the end of the first-half, Cesc passed to Oscar. From a midfield position, Eden burst forward and Oscar backheeled it perfectly for him. He ran into the penalty area and coolly put the ball through goalkeeper David de Gea's legs.

Eden slid on his knees towards the fans with his arms out wide. He was the hero again and the fans were chanting his name as loudly as they could. It was a brilliant goal by 'the new Eden' – hard work, speed and skill in one world-class player. There was just no stopping him now.

That goal was the winner and one of the most important that he had ever scored. Mourinho gave him a big hug as he left the field.

'Eden is one of the three best players in the world,' the Chelsea manager told the press. 'He has a lot of responsibility now but he is doing a fantastic job. He deserves to win the Premier League and the Player of the Year award.'

It was a great feeling to hear that from one of the best managers in the world. Eden was named in the PFA Team of the Year and he was also the strong favourite to win the PFA Player of the Year award. He had competition from Philippe Coutinho, David de Gea, Harry Kane, Alexis Sánchez and Diego Costa but Eden had more assists than any other player as well as fifteen goals. Everyone was comparing him to Messi and Ronaldo, and Mourinho even joked that each of his legs was worth £100 million.

Eden had won lots of awards in France but the prospect of this one was extra special. He was nervous as he sat in his smart suit at the ceremony in London's Grosvenor Hotel. Luckily, a lot of his Chelsea teammates were there to take his mind off things as he waited for the news. It would be a great honour if the players voted for him as the best player of the season. Finally, it was the moment they were all waiting for.

'This year's PFA Player of the Year is...' the presenter began. '...Chelsea's Eden Hazard!'

Eden had a big smile on his face as he went up on stage to collect the huge trophy. He was so pleased to win the same award as amazing players like Thierry Henry and Luis Suárez.

'I'm very happy,' he told the audience. 'One day I want to be the best and this season I've played very well and so have Chelsea. Thank you for this award!'

Eden enjoyed the moment but then got ready to finish his job. Two weeks later, Chelsea became Premier League champions, and who scored the winning goal against Crystal Palace? Eden, of course. At the final whistle, the Chelsea players hugged each other and danced. Eden was their star player but it had been an amazing team effort.

'We've done it!' Eden shouted to Cesc. 'We're champions!'

The real celebrations came three weeks later, after their final game of the season against Sunderland. The team came back on to the pitch for the presentation, with Mourinho at the front. Eden got one of the loudest cheers of all when they called his name. Once he had received his medal, he stood in the front row with Oscar and Cesc making lots and lots of noise. As John lifted the Premier League trophy, they all jumped up and down. Everyone in the stadium was singing together:

'*Champione, Champione, Ole Ole Ole!*'

The trophy was passed around the players and when it reached Eden, he lifted it high into the air and then kissed it. It was so nice to have his whole family there in the crowd to share his big day. Their love and encouragement was so important to him.

'There's nothing left for you to achieve in England!' Thorgan joked. 'Do you still dream of playing for Real Madrid?'

'I enjoy my football here and I have the chance to win trophies,' Eden replied. 'It would be silly to change. I haven't won the Champions League or the *Ballon D'Or* yet!'

'But no-one gets kicked as much as you do,' Kylian argued. 'You leave the field after every game with so many cuts and bruises.'

'That's just how football is here in Britain – people like a battle. I don't mind, I can take the hits like a boxer now!'

Eden had worked so hard to win the title and

become the consistent superstar that Mourinho knew he could be. In one amazing season, he had won the League Cup, the Premier League, the PFA Player of the Year and the Football Writers' Association Player of the Year.

'What a year!' he said to Natacha as they relaxed at home with Yannis and Leo. 'Can it get any better than that?'

His wife laughed. 'With you, things usually just get better and better. What's next?'

Eden knew the answer to that. 'More winners' medals, of course!'

Turn the page for a sneak preview of
another brilliant football story by
Matt and Tom Oldfield. . .

ALEXIS SANCHEZ

Available now!

CHAPTER 1

WINNING AT WEMBLEY

'Alexis Sánchez baby, Alexis Sánchez
oooohhhhhhhh!'

Alexis could hear the Arsenal fans loud and clear as
he warmed up on the Wembley pitch. He loved the
song that they had made for him. There was still half
an hour until kick-off but the atmosphere was already
amazing. It was Arsenal's second FA Cup Final in a
row but for Alexis, this was the chance to win a first
English trophy, and what a trophy it was. Even as a
kid growing up in Chile, Alexis knew about the oldest
football competition in the world. It was a dream
come true.

'Alexis, this is it,' Arsène Wenger said to him in the

dressing room before the game, but he knew he didn't really need to inspire his superstar. 'You've had an amazing first year here but you need to end it with a winner's medal!'

As Alexis walked out on to the pitch, holding the hand of a mascot, fireworks went off all over the pitch. The FA Cup trophy was sitting there, shining brightly and waiting for him. He couldn't wait to get the ball and run at the Aston Villa defence. He knew it would be a tough game but there was no way he was going to lose this match. Alexis had been the Arsenal hero in the semi-final, scoring both goals to beat Reading. And he was determined to be the hero again in the final.

'We need to stay focused and we need to be patient,' Alexis said to Mesut Özil and Theo Walcott, his partners in attack. 'If we play well, we will score in the end.'

Alexis was right. Aston Villa stopped them again and again but the Gunners didn't give up or get frustrated. At the end of the first half, the Gunners finally scored and it was thanks to Alexis. Nacho Monreal crossed from the left and Alexis was there at the back post. He couldn't get enough power to head for goal so instead he headed the ball across to Theo, who smashed it into the back of the net. They had that goal they needed.

'I'm not done yet,' Alexis told Mesut once Arsène had given his half-time team talk. The important message was that they were only halfway to victory. 'I want to win but I also want to score!'

Five minutes into the second half, Alexis chased across the pitch to get to the ball first. The Aston Villa defenders backed away in fear of what he might do with his brilliant skill. Alexis had the space he needed for one of his trademark long-range shots. With his right foot, he hit the ball with so much power and swerve that the goalkeeper could do nothing as it sailed over his head. Alexis couldn't believe it; he had scored and it was one of his best goals ever.

Per Mertesacker scored a third and Olivier Giroud made it four. 4–0 – what a way to win the FA Cup Final! On the touchline, Arsène clapped and allowed himself to smile. He was very proud of his squad and especially his Chilean superstar. What a signing he had been.

'Arsenal! Arsenal! Arsenal!' Alexis shouted with his teammates at the final whistle. They were a close group of friends and they were in the mood for a party.

With an Arsenal scarf around his neck and a Chilean flag in his hands, Alexis was one of the first players to walk up the stadium steps to collect his medal from Prince William. As he passed, the fans high-fived him and patted him on the back. He was part of the Arsenal family now and he loved it. It was great to get the medal but what he really wanted was the trophy. Captains Per and Mikel Arteta were the first to lift it and then it was his turn.

Alexis shouted for joy as he raised it above his head. He kissed it twice and passed it on to Jack Wilshere.

'We did it!' Jack told him, giving him a big hug. He was wearing a silly red-and-white jester hat and he was having the time of his life.

It wasn't Alexis's first trophy but it was certainly one of his favourites. Down on the pitch, there were more fireworks and Theo sprayed champagne everywhere. The players thanked the fans by having selfies taken with them. It was a really great celebration. Alexis wished that his family and friends could have come from Chile to share his special day but they had all sent him good luck messages.

It was an incredible way to end the best season of his career so far. Twenty-five goals and twelve assists was a new record for Alexis. The big-money transfer from Barcelona had put a lot of pressure on him to perform. He had worked really hard and the players and fans had made him feel so welcome. Arsenal Football Club felt like home and he was already excited about challenging for more trophies next year.

'Let's win the Premier League and the Champions League!' Alexis told Mesut as they posed for more photos.

He had come a long way from Tocopilla.

Lille

🏆 Ligue 1: 2010 – 11

🏆 Coup de France: 2010 – 11

Chelsea

🏆 Premier League: 2014 – 15

🏆 Football League Cup: 2014 – 15

🏆 UEFA Europa League (2): 2012 – 13,
2018 – 2019

Individual

🏆 UNFP Ligue 1 Player of the Year (2): 2010 – 11,
2011 – 12

🏆 UNFP Ligue 1 Young Player of the Year (2):
2008 – 09, 2009 – 10

🏆 UNFP Ligue 1 Team of the Year (3): 2009 – 10,
2010 – 11, 2011 – 12

🏆 UNFP Player of the Month (3): March 2010,
March 2011, March 2012

🏆 Premier League Player of the Season: 2014 – 15

🏆 FWA Footballer of the Year: 2014 – 15

🏆 PFA Players' Player of the Year: 2014 – 15

🏆 PFA Young Player of the Year: 2013 – 2014

🏆 PFA Team of the Year (4): 2012 – 13, 2013 – 14,
2014 – 15, 2016 – 2017

🏆 ESM Team of the Year: 2014 – 15

🏆 Chelsea Player of the Year (4): 2013 – 2014,
2014 – 15, 2016 – 2017, 2018 – 2019

🏆 Chelsea Players' Player of the Year (2): 2014 – 15,
2018 – 2019

🏆 Bravo Award: 2011

🏆 FIFA World Cup Silver Ball: 2018

🏆 Belgian Sportsman of the Year: 2018

HAZARD

23 **THE FACTS**

NAME: Eden Michael Hazard

DATE OF BIRTH: 7 January 1991

AGE: 28

PLACE OF BIRTH: La Louvière

NATIONALITY: Belgium

BEST FRIEND: Christian Benteke

CURRENT CLUB: Real Madrid

POSITION: LM

THE STATS

Height (cm):	173
Club appearances:	546
Club goals:	160
Club trophies:	6
International appearances:	102
International goals:	30
International trophies:	0
Ballon d'Ors:	0

★ ★ ★ **HERO RATING: 89** ★ ★ ★

GREATEST MOMENTS

15 NOVEMBER 2008, LILLE 3-0 SAINT-ÉTIENNE

This was Eden's first ever league start and the seventeen-year-old really made the most of his opportunity. In the twenty-fifth minute, Eden dribbled at the right-back. Three step-overs later, he curled a shot into the bottom corner. With skills like that, Eden was soon a regular starter for Lille.

11 MARCH 2010, LILLE 1-0 LIVERPOOL

Eden was already a young star in France and Belgium but this match-winning Europa League performance against Liverpool grabbed England's attention too. With five minutes to go, his free-kick flew over the wall and bounced down into the bottom corner. That season, Lille won the French League and Cup Double, and Eden was named Ligue 1 Player of the Year.

4 DECEMBER 2013, SUNDERLAND 3-4 CHELSEA

Under new manager José Mourinho, Eden got better and better at Chelsea. This Premier League match against Sunderland was a sign of the great things to come. After setting up the first goal for Frank Lampard, Eden scored two brilliant goals of his own. He finished the season as Chelsea's top scorer.

22 JUNE 2014, BELGIUM 1-0 RUSSIA

Eden isn't just a goalscorer; he also creates goals with his awesome dribbling. The 2014 World Cup in Brazil was his first big international tournament and he was Belgium's hero against Russia. With two minutes to go, Eden ran down the left wing and played a perfect pass for Divock Origi to score. Belgium made it to the quarter-finals.

3 MAY 2015, CHELSEA 1-0 CRYSTAL PALACE

Eden was the best player in the Premier League during the 2014-15 season. Against Crystal Palace, he won the title for Chelsea in dramatic style. Eden won a penalty after a great dribble into the box. His spot-kick was saved but he scored the rebound with a rare header. It was his nineteenth goal of the season.

PLAY LIKE YOUR HEROES

THE EDEN HAZARD
RABONA

STEP 1: Dribble down the right wing with your right foot.

STEP 2: If the left-back tries to push you out wide, drag the back with a nice Cruyff turn.

STEP 3: You're now on your weaker left foot – or that's what the defenders think anyway! But instead, plant your left foot and swing your right foot round so that it's the other side of your left.

STEP 4: With as much power as possible, chip the ball with the front of your right foot. Aim for the six-yard box and the head of your star striker.

STEP 5: Or if you're feeling really confident, and the goal isn't too far away, take a shot!

STEP 6: Don't celebrate too much. You're a cool, classy playmaker, after all.

TEST YOUR KNOWLEDGE

QUESTIONS

1. What positions did Eden's parents play on the football pitch?

2. How many teams did Eden play for before he joined Lille?

3. Who were Eden's top two childhood football heroes?

4. Which Belgian legend did Eden impress when he was fourteen, and which superstar did he compare Eden to?

5. How old was Eden when he moved from Belgium to France?

6. Which Lille manager gave Eden his first-team debut in November 2007?

7. What was the name of Eden's favourite pizza restaurant in Lille and what was the name of the owner?

8. What are Eden's favourite sports, other than football?

9. How many team and individual trophies did Eden win at Lille?

10. How old was Eden when he joined Chelsea and which other English club did he turn down?

11. Which Chelsea manager helped Eden to become a superstar Number 10?

Answers below. . . No cheating!

1. *Carine was a striker and Thierry was a defensive midfielder.*
2. *2 – Royal Stade Brainois and Tubize.* 3. *Ronaldinho and Zinedine Zidane.* 4. *It was Enzo Scifo and he compared Eden to Thierry Henry.*
5. *He was 14 when he joined the Lille academy.* 6. *Claude Puel.*
7. *It was called Ristorante al Ritrovo and Pino was the owner.* 8. *Table tennis and basketball.* 9. *6 – 2 team trophies (Ligue 1 and French Cup) and 4 individual trophies (2 x Ligue 1 Young Player of the Year award and 2 x Ligue 1 Player of the Year award).* 10. *Eden was 21 and he chose Chelsea over Manchester United.* 11. *José Mourinho.*

HAVE YOU GOT THEM ALL?

ULTIMATE FOOTBALL HEROES